A CRISIS OF COMPETENCE

How our education system is failing kids and what to do about it

Dr. Clarence Nixon Jr.

Published by HigherLife Development Services, Inc.
PO Box 623307
Oviedo, FL 32762
(407) 563-4806
www.ahigherlife.com

ISBN: 978-1-958211-58-8 (hardback)
ISBN: 978-1-958211-12-0 (paperback)
ISBN: 978-1-958211-13-7 (ebook)
Library of Congress case no. 2023909413

Printed in the United States of America
10 9 8 7 6 5 4 3 2 1

DEDICATION

This book is dedicated to my wife, Robin Nixon, family, friends, and staff. I am especially grateful for the late Bishop B.A. Gibert and his remarkable example of excellence, anointing, teaching, and wisdom that touched so many lives in transformational ways. My sincerest gratitude extends to Kathleen Valencia for being supportive and insightful in completing this book.

I pray that this book will be a blessing to parents, students, and educators alike as they set out on their journey toward educational competence. May it serve as a guide and empower them with the knowledge they need to attain success. May all who read it gain wisdom and insight from its contents. Thank you for your commitment to excellence and for being part of this remarkable endeavor!

This book is a testament to the dedication and hard work of many. It is my sincere hope that it will positively impact lives and make a lasting difference in our education system. Thank you all for your excellence, wisdom, and insight!

CONTENTS

CONTENTS

FOREWORD

This book, *A Crisis of Competence*, is a brilliant call to action for those who care about the future of our nation's educational system. Through analysis of relevant metrics and statistics, it paints a sobering picture of systemic failure within urban America, which has led to an imbalance in educational outcomes that disproportionally affect African American students.

Thankfully, t.Lab has stepped up to begin restoring balance and promoting superb competence among our nation's students, particularly those from urban areas.

Through the use of technology-enabled processes and anointed and competent teaching professionals, t.Lab has provided a beacon of hope in these dark days of fallen standards, broken promises, and failed opportunities. With so much riding on the future success of our students, *A Crisis of Competence* serves as a reminder that the time for action is now and success is possible. We must work together to create an educational environment where all children can realize their potential.

We owe it to t.Lab and this book for providing a remarkable roadmap for us to follow. By following this pathway, we can finally begin to restore our educational system and ensure a brighter future for generations of students to come. It's time we embrace this challenge and make competence in education a reality. Let's start now!

Sincerely,
Attorney John W. Daniels Jr.
May 2, 2023

ACKNOWLEDGMENTS

I am truly blessed to have Bishop Andrew Merritt and Pastor Viveca Merritt, Elders John and Dale Henderson, and Pastors Gerald and Lynn Johnson in my life. They are spiritual role models who embody excellence and serve as living examples of Kings and Priests. I can't thank them enough for their unwavering support, guidance, and direction over the years. Their collective wisdom and experience have been a major driving force behind t.Lab and the Drive to 25 initiatives. Without them, we wouldn't be where we are today. I'm grateful for all that they do and am excited to see how far we can go with their continued support!

Thank you!

Dr. Clarence Nixon Jr.

Author of *A Crisis of Competence*

Founder and CEO, t.Lab

INTRODUCTION

Our education system is failing.

I know that is a strong statement. I know that not everyone will agree. I also want to do more than state an argument to prove failure. This book provides a case for appropriate and needed change. This book presents new possibilities and methods which can offer solutions. This book shows how and why the present system is not succeeding, which students are left out, and what can be done to shift those trends.

We all know that not everything always works well.

We also know that when something isn't working well we need to adjust, to adapt, to shift, to change.

We also know that such drastic changes can be slow and difficult and almost impossible.

But even if when change is hard, we must adjust and adapt if the proposed outcomes are of great value. So it is with the education of our children.

Our younger generations are of huge value. They will determine our future. And, I believe, our methods of educating and mentoring them are determining their futures—and therefore our own.

Unfortunately, the present systems of shaping those who will guide our future are not working. It must change. Not just in theory. Not just for some new trend. Not just policy and procedure. But measurable, practical, and successful changes in how we educate our youth.

I offer those possibilities in this book, and this chapter helps you understand what is driving us and what should drive us. Through years of seeing what works, I ask you to consider these principles. Students who had felt hopeless now see success. Students who were looked down on by educational structure or given favor as an acceptable means of not challenging them to believe in themselves are now confident after hard work through new methods of learning.

Join me. Read these thoughts and ideas and examples, and join me. They are working. They are working for me and for many students. They can work for you.

Refuse to remain stuck in unsuccessful forms of education and transformation. Bring change. Our students need it. Our culture needs it. Our world needs it.

Now is your chance.

Now is our chance.

CHAPTER 1

WHY A CRISIS?

Then the LORD replied: "Write down the revelation and
make it plain on tablets so that a herald may run with it."
Habakkuk 2:2 NIV

The academic competence of American students is decreasing.
Their instruction lacks excellence. Their vision for the future
is weak. Their study skills are not adequate for the global marketplace. American students are falling behind.

While COVID-19 responses highlighted and exacerbated the
obstacles our students face, it was not the cause. The pandemic
does, however, give us impetus to incorporate technology into education delivery. The end result: increased student competence.

Educational competence is measurable—and decreasing.
Academic competence is measured by well-established bench-
marks such as the American College Test, known by its acronym,
ACT.

Standardized testing has its detractors. I disagree strongly. In
this book, I will validate its usefulness. A standardized test does
have limitations; for example, it does not measure competence
outside the core educational subjects. The student's competence
in character, digital skills, cultural acuity, and mental health are not
measured by ACT and Scholastic Aptitude Tests (SAT).

The coming chapters reveal why the ACT, and its counterpart the SAT, are good measures of competence. We will dissect the issues that influence students' scores on these tests. Our nation's lackluster results have contributing causes which we shall analyze.

Finally, we will explore what's needed to make a change. Our goal is to ensure that every student achieves competence. Only then will our society be changed.

In a nutshell, this book, *A Crisis of Competence*, reveals the current educational product of incompetent students and identifies the changes needed for universal student competence.

The number of students without competence for higher education is increasing. Before the onset of COVID-19 in early 2020, colleges and universities had already begun to change ACT and SAT requirements from their admission standards. These tests reveal the competence level of a student in the core subjects: English, Mathematics, Reading, Science, and Writing. Such standardized tests validate the skill level of a student and project the probability of their success in the first two years of college.

That probability is decreasing for all but one group. In 2016, only about a third of high school students were college-ready. (https://www.usnews.com/news/articles/2016-04-27/high-school-seniors-arent-college-ready-naep-data-show accessed 10-27). Simultaneously, students' average grades in core classes are increasing. More A grades are given than ever before. In the coming pages, we analyze this unexpected contradiction to reveal the true decline in the competence of American students.

A system to create success is required—and there is one. My organization is t.Lab, short for Technology lab. I am the founder of t.Lab as well as a doctoral level adjunct professor. We have proven that it produces competence in students.

We are a faith-enabled accelerated learning center. Our center aims to improve the academic excellence among our student base in grades prekindergarten through undergraduate levels. Our national initiative, *The Drive to 25*, aims to increase the median ACT scores of African American students from the current 16.1 (where 36 is the highest) to 25, by year end 2025.

As the leader of t.Lab, I see the myriad issues affecting the scores. They are well understood in our analyses and programs. But whatever the influences may be, the student is left incompetent for reaching their potential. They are not ready for college, nor are they prepared to contribute significantly to our society.

Any race can realize high ACT scores; ethnicity is no excuse for failure to do so. We have succeeded in raising median scores for the students we influence. Our success at t.Lab has consistently proven the ability of African American students to perform well above the ACT competence benchmark of 21.25.

Every student can and should achieve competence. It is not happening now. I wrote this book, *A Crisis of Competence*, to reverse the trend toward incompetence.

In 2018, 35 percent of high school graduates met none of the ACT College Readiness Benchmarks. This is a trend; more students yearly fail to have a measurable proficiency in core educational subjects. The 35% in 2018 was an increase from 33% in 2017 and 31% in 2014. (ACT 1/1/21 http://www.act.org/content/dam/act/unsecured/documents/cccr2018/National-CCCR-2018.pdf)

In 2019, ACT headlines confirmed again the downward trend in college readiness. "Decline in College Readiness Continues Among United States High School Grads, New ACT Report Finds." The report reads in part:

Overall, 37 percent of ACT-tested graduates in the class of 2019 met at least three of the four ACT College Readiness

Benchmarks (English, reading, math, and science), showing strong college readiness. This is down slightly from 38 percent last year and 39 percent in 2017.

However, nearly as many—36 percent—did not meet any of the four benchmarks, a number that has increased over the past several years. (https://leadershipblog.act.org/2019/10/decline-in-college-readiness-continues.html accessed 1/1/21)

The decrease in American students' test scores is across the board, except for Asian students. Scores measure academic competence. Faring the worst are African American students. This decline is evident among Americans of European descent as well, who trail Asian scores more than the standard deviation of 2.5—a sign of falling behind.

The performance of Hispanic, American Indian, and African American students on the ACT is an important indicator for educational success in the US. Understanding how these groups have performed over time with respect to the composite score, benchmarks, and standard deviation can help us gain insight into the progress of our educational system.

Over the past five years, the performance of Hispanic and American Indian students on the ACT has been trending positively. The average composite score for Hispanics has consistently increased during this period, while the average composite score for American Indians has remained stable. Furthermore, both groups have shown marked improvements in reaching ACT benchmarks.

Performance of African American students on the ACT has been trending negatively over the same period. The average composite score for African Americans has steadily decreased during this time and there have been relative declines in overall benchmarks achieved by this group. Furthermore, standard deviation scores for African Americans are also lower than the other two groups.

If we are to make meaningful progress, we must take steps to ensure equitable access to quality education for all students. The United States is the world's leader in providing and maintaining educational capacity. Each student must be held accountable to leverage the resources available to them.

How then can a Fordham Institute study find that an *increasing* number of students are receiving A grades in their high school classes? These same students have decreasing scores on the standardized tests.

Certainly, standardized tests like the ACT are not perfect. They do not predict a student's future or determine their limits. Such tests are, however, an effective tool to measure competence at a point in time. At t.Lab, we believe that all students in any ethnic group or race can perform at the ACT benchmark of 21.25, and above.

However, a significant change in paradigm, processes, systems, and leadership is required for that to occur.

The evidence for our belief is global. Programme for International Student Assessment (PISA) scores measure reading competence in countries like China, South Korea, and India. There, the 2018 PISA results showed a rise in competence. The contrast with the decline of American students' competence is unnerving.

Project the above facts forward. It is clear that America is at risk. Without changes now to increase student competence, those born from 1996 to 2015 (*a.k.a.* Gen Z) will lose in global job competition. With less competence, American students will be ill prepared to win jobs and command higher incomes.

Statistics now show that more Asians are immigrating and entering the US to attend medical school. Simultaneously, medical school admission standards are lowered for African American students. These contrasting realities are a signal that American educational systems leave American students incompetent for higher education and professional careers. [https://www.thefp.com/p/the-inside-forces-upending-medicine]

The COVID pandemic exposed the systemic failure in American education. The drive to produce exceptional students is lacking. The vision to imagine every student competent has been disincentivized. Our national security is diminishing as a result, as we shall discuss.

It is up to all stakeholders—parents, educational leaders, and all Americans—to put our best team on the field. Our students can be the global leaders in every industry if we will reverse our contributions to their incompetence and low test scores.

The cliché is true: education begins at home. Parents are the first and the primary educators of children. Without parental initiative, a critical gap arises between the potential and the competence of their children. Parents aid in a child's character formation, which is integral to the child's future leadership footprint. From parents, children learn a host of essential character qualities, such as love of learning, determination to excel, and drive to improve. Children who learn to challenge themselves and others widen their leadership footprint.

God considers the parent's role so critical for a child's future, He tells them to teach the children "morning, noon, and night." For the child, it is critical that parents accept and continue their God-given responsibility and reclaim the responsibility they may have forfeited.

Parents rely upon professional educators, who are not embracing the need for radical change. COVID-related challenges are often blamed, but our students' test scores were declining long before.

Education industry leaders are wrong to dismiss this and defend existing systems ,which are proven to produce incompetence. Curriculum specifically designed to increase student competence must be implemented. Consistent measurement with consistent standards can enable consistent results.

Now parents, educators, and all stakeholders must work together if we are to have any hope of reversing years of decline in American student competence.

What will such a change look like? How will it contrast with the current activity in American students' homes and schools? This book holds a blueprint which I formed using my experience, education, and significant market exposure. Professional years as an information technology systems engineer and as a management professional with success in turnaround prepared me for the analyses in this book and the prescriptions it contains.

As creator of t.Lab and as an adjunct professor, I offer the reader a reality check on our current system producing incompetent students. I propose a paradigm shift for parents and leaders. These enable the turnaround of America's educational decline. My solution ensures a growth for our position in the world by producing students who are drivers and influences of both industry and peace.

As you read *A Crisis of Competence*, you will see we'll explore the causes of the substandard American educational product. Our core message is the effective and proven model of t.Lab, which justifies the new paradigm I am advocating.

Both today and tomorrow, student character is the foundation. Upon it, we enable rapid advance in competence for math, science, and digital technology. America must be the global leader as global economic demand rapidly changes. This requires student competence.

A Crisis of Competence provides parents, educational leaders, and stakeholders a window on decreasing competence, as measured by secondary and postsecondary tests. This book presents the truth and the methods needed in children's education, to unite Americans for success both at home and in global competition.

I am not writing about race or politics, although they comprise numerous examples. For authentic assessment of our educational challenges, political and racial causes must be included. Yet we cannot afford to wait for any party, official, or bureaucrat to make the changes required to reverse our trend of declining competence. Parents and educational leaders must honestly face the crisis and accept the costs of our current descent path.

I founded and continue to lead t.Lab. We have long recognized the crisis of competence. In 2019 we initiated a national project branded DRIVE TO 25. Its goal is raising African American median ACT scores to 25 by 2025.

Our drive targets one ethnic group but is open to all. At t.Lab, we work with both domestic and international students; many races and ethnicities are represented.

Yet because of America's unique history and the US caste system, African Americans will need to compete and outperform other students just to be considered peers of students from other races and ethnicities. Competence is critical in this ethnic group, which is performing at the lowest level. In 2022, the median score of African Americans was 16.1.

Educational and cultural competence is paramount in destroying caste systems as well as a paradigm shift, new development systems, and a significant dose of competitiveness will cure the woes of incompetence.

Please accept my humble offer from my informed, experienced, and proven perspective, *A Crisis of Competence.* In these pages are insights that every American educator, parent, and stakeholder can embrace, leading our students and children to new levels of competence, outpacing the world.

As John F. Kennedy said, "A rising tide raises all boats." It is time to rise.

CHAPTER 2

THE COSTS OF INCOMPETENCE

Each tree is recognized by its own fruit.
Luke 6:44

Incompetence is a failure to deliver and meet a performance standard or requirement.

When have you been impacted by a lack of competence? Perhaps the loss was time, money, a relationship, or security. In their place arises anxiety and sorrow.

When did a lack of knowledge hurt? Perhaps it involved someone unwilling to learn and lacking understanding. Concern for others can be absent, enervating motivation to gain competence. A person who lacks ability may want to achieve competence yet be unable to.

Consider the US Capitol riot following the November 2020 election as an example. The missing element was competent leadership and character. Rioters who stormed the Capitol included business leaders and owners, off-duty police officers, and many with positions or responsibility. Clearly, neither a college degree nor knowledge level alone provide competence, which stems from strong character.

A tree is judged by the fruit that it bears. Self-control, honesty, and respect are all attributes of strong character, which produces good leadership skills. The violence at the Capitol was perpetrated by Americans who lack competence.

In education, it's easy to see the lack of academic competence. They are evident in the ACT and SAT scores. Predictably, the scores of a host of postsecondary standardized test scores affirm the decrease: the MCAT, LSAT, DAT, GRE, GAT, to name only a few.

The issue of competence encompasses everything: how we treat one another, personal integrity, thoughtfulness for others, decision-making, product design, and service excellence. Incompetence is often associated with poor character, which together produce social instability. In contrast, the outcome of competence is a better society.

Too often, though, we see less of that outcome. What about subject knowledge competence?

Our Decreasing Competence

Being called competent is not usually a descriptor a student hopes to receive from a teacher. To be competent means to be average in their minds, a "C" on a report card. Most students I work with hope to be described as exemplary, superior, or excellent, manifested as an A in a class.

These are misconceptions and inaccurate definitions of "competent." Competence is doing something successfully and effectively all the time and meeting requirements and standards.

Students receive high grades for schoolwork—As and Bs—in greater proportion than ever before. Whether these high grades are justified is another question. The current grading practices leave a lot to be desired. Competence by definition would mean that a student mastered all of the requirements in a course. Any grade below an A should mean that the student was operating with some incompetence.

The ACT benchmark score for competence for college is 21.25. The student with such a score or higher is qualified for college. Statistics show that, in the first two years of college, students with a 21.25 ACT score have a 75% chance of receiving a C grade or better, and a 50% chance of a B or better. The benchmark 21.25 is not the exceptional student.

ACT Performance Across Ethnicities

Yet recent years show a decreasing number of American students able to achieve that middle-of-the-road score. Consider the following table. These scores represent the average score of all four core subjects. (*Source:* https://blog.prepscholar.com/average-act-score-by-year.)

ACT Composite Scores 2019 through 2022:

Ethnicities	2019	2020	2021	2022
White	22.1	22.0	21.7	21.3
African American	16.8	16.7	16.3	16.1
Asian American	24.6	24.6	24.9	24.7
Hispanics	18.7	18.5	18.3	17.7

Any student's performance on the ACT is an important indicator for educational success in the US. Understanding how these subgroups have performed over time with respect to the composite score, benchmarks, and standard deviation reveals the progress of our educational system—or lack thereof.

Performance of African American students on the ACT has been trending negatively over the same period. The median composite score for African Americans has steadily decreased during this time and there have been relative declines in overall benchmarks achieved by this group. Furthermore, standard deviation scores for African Americans are also lower than the other groups.

It is clear that differences in performance still exist between racial and ethnic groups in terms of educational performance on the ACT. If we are to make meaningful progress, we must take steps to ensure that all students can take advantage of the opportunities that exist. It is not a money issue. Parents and students are not using the opportunities available to them. The USA leads the PISA nations in education capacity.

PREJUDICE AND INCOMPETENCE

In today's society, prejudice and incompetence are two major factors that can lead to social instability. Discrimination limits opportunities for many individuals from minorities or those in under-privileged socio-economic situations, leading to tension and even violence between different groups. Similarly, academic incompetence can lead to a lack of critical thinking skills among citizens, which can easily be exploited by malicious individuals or organizations looking to destabilize society.

Discrimination has been a long-standing issue in modern society, and its effects have only become more apparent as the years go on. From job opportunities being limited based on gender or race to unequal access to education based on financial background, discrimination continues to keep certain groups of people out of power while allowing others to thrive. This leads to resentment and frustration among those in the disadvantaged group, which can easily boil over into social unrest.

In addition, academic incompetence is a major issue that can lead to widespread instability. As citizens become less educated, they are more likely to be swayed by false information or radical ideas that seek to undermine democratic values and rights. Furthermore, more people with high-quality education leads to

greater economic stability as well as critical thinking skills necessary for understanding complex issues such as civil rights, healthcare reform, and other policies related to the effective governing of
society.

It is clear that both discrimination and academic incompetence
have a large impact on social stability across the world today. It
is, therefore, essential for governments, non-governmental organizations, and individuals alike to work together toward eliminating
these issues in order to create a more stable, equitable society.
By tackling discrimination and academic incompetence head-on,
we can ensure that all citizens have an equal chance at success
while also keeping our societies safe from those who would seek
to destabilize them. This is the only way forward if we are to truly
achieve social stability. Only then can we truly move toward a level
playing field for in the US education system.

In reality a broad range and alarming number of American
students are unable to achieve a "competent" composite score
on standardized tests—even while their classwork grades are
increasing.

INCREASING DISPARITY OF GRADES AND COMPETENCE

Concurrent with decreasing ACT scores for high school graduates,
schoolwork grades are increasing. In fact, they are higher than
ever before. In 2018, the Fordham Institute hosted a discussion
titled, "Inflated Grades: What Happens When Report Cards Lie?"

Inflated grades are occurring across the nation. While ACT and
SAT scores are dropping, the A's given to students are increasing.
A is the grade given most, 52 or 53 percent of the time. And to
accommodate decreasing test scores, some colleges are dropping
the testing requirement for admission, but this neither promotes
the competition American students need to realize nor pushes the
educational system to build competencies.

However, we believe that grades can be closely aligned with competency when grades are not inflated. In 2009, Pearson, a multinational education provider, identified a close correlation between grade point averages (GPA) and ACT scores. The research established that students with a GPA of 2.0 or better were likely to realize the ACT benchmark of 21.25 or better. Those students with GPAs of 3.0 or better all realized ACT scores of 30 or better, placing them on the top 5% of students taking the ACT. See appendix A.

This is a reality I see almost daily. Just recently, t.Lab enrolled two new high school students into our program. Both have GPAs of 4.2 and 3.5, and realized ACT scores of 14.75 and 15.25, respectively. Two other students, both attendees of a top high school in a major urban city, realized GPAs of 3.0 and 2.8 while realizing composite ACT scores of 17.5 and 13.25, respectively. Both the latter two students were accepted into three major universities and/ or colleges whose median entering class ACT scores ranged from 27 to 28.

Remember, 21.25 is the benchmark score that establishes that students can do college work at the freshman and sophomore levels. While both of these students certainly can succeed, they enter behind their classmates in academic competence, which will make success more difficult for them, having both less knowledge and the ability to apply knowledge sufficiently than many of their peers.

Additionally, we use IXL to establish the grade operating level or competency of students seeking to join t.Lab. IXL is a web-based portal that provides the ability to assess student performance levels from first grade through twelfth grade in multiple disciplines, including Math, Language Arts, and Reading. IXL is a highly accurate and reliable tool for determining student performance levels and competence.

It has been our experience that students who realized ACT scores at 16.1 tend to realize performance levels at the second, third, and fourth grade levels. This is a disturbing occurrence because often these students have high grade point averages of 3.0 and above. The reality of grade inflation is a significant factor in transforming the performance of all students but especially African American students, as the following scatter plot demonstrates graphically.

Result 1: Scatter Plot ACT vs. GPA

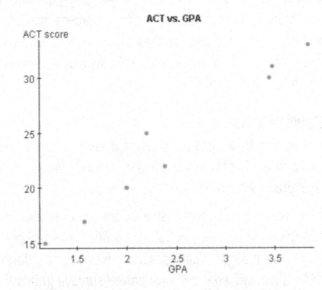

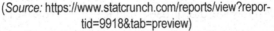

(*Source:* https://www.statcrunch.com/reports/view?reportid=9918&tab=preview)

This trend is occurring nationwide. A 2018 study by the Fordham Institute revealed of all North Carolina High School Algebra 1 students who received an A in the course, only a fifth of those receiving A's reached a superior level on the Algebra 1 end of course exam. Only 81 percent of those receiving A's were ready for college. Only 43 percent of students receiving Bs met the college-ready level for Algebra. This means a majority of B-receiving students did not meet the college-ready level standards. More than a third of B-receiving students did not meet the proficiency standard for high school Algebra. In effect, these students failed high school Algebra—even though they received a B in the class.

The Fordham study also looked at GPAs in North Carolina over an eleven-year period and found that GPAs increased for both more and less affluent schools during the eleven years included in the study. Even more, the results indicated that while GPAs increased in both groups, GPAs of more affluent schools increased more than the GPAs at the less affluent schools' GPAs. The gap between the less and more affluent students in North Carolina actually grew during this period. This tells us that grade inflation is more pronounced in more affluent schools. (The GPAs studied were the full GPAs for all of high school.)

MISLEADING PARENTS

A parent seeing their child's A's and 4.0 GPA believes they are ready for college. But the Fordham study sounds the alarm on the subject of grade inflation in the following excerpt.

> According to National Assessment of Educational Progress results, only about a third of US high school seniors are academically prepared for postsecondary education. Yet we know from parent surveys [(https:// bealearninghero.org/research/] that 90 percent of parents believe their children are performing at grade level. In Washington D.C., recent scandals [https:// www.npr.org/sections/ed/2018/01/29/581036306/ in-d-c-thirty-four-percent-of-graduates-received-a-diploma-against-district-poli] revealed that teachers felt pressured to give passing grades to failing students to boost graduation rates, while recent research [https://

www.usatoday.com/story/news/2017/07/17/easy-a-
nearly-half-hs-seniors-graduate-average/485787001/]
shows that schools in more affluent communities have
seen gaps between GPAs and test scores grow more
than have other schools. All of which seems to suggest that grades are unreliable signals of academic
success and college readiness.

If report cards overstate student learning, they can
trigger a vicious cycle of underachievement, promoting ill-prepared students and forestalling needed interventions that could get them back on track. Whether it
means conferring a gentlemen's C to a failing student
or bumping a B to an A for an above-average one,
inflated grades give parents, students, and colleges
false information about content mastery, potentially
pushing graduates to choose postsecondary options
they are not prepared for and colleges to make admission decisions based on data that favor students
from particular schools. (Source: *https://nces.ed.gov/
nationsreportcard/*)

Because so many students receive As, parents believe their children are performing well, that they are on track and even excelling
in core subjects. This is not the case, as often standardized test
scores prove.

Inflated grades create an altered perception for parents and
students. If a student receives an A, more studying is not needed—right? If a parent sees a child's report card shows all or mostly
As, then Mom or Dad believes their child is doing well. Inflated
grades create a false impression that too often is not discovered
until a child takes the ACT or SAT or even enters college, as some
schools do not require standardized test scores.

Today, more than ever before, parents must be proactive in respect to their children's' education. They must educate themselves on these alarming trends so their children can excel in school and thus succeed in their future careers. In chapter seven we'll take a deeper look at parenting—a primary asset for growing competence.

DECREASING COMPETENCE TO WORK AND EARN

While competence is decreasing, the demand for skills in higher-level math and science is growing. Decreasing student competence in every level of our education system provides a glimpse into the future. American students have a diminishing competence to lead tomorrow.

The ACT scores reveal that more and more US students are simply not competent.

Corporate America has recognized the competence decline as well. After witnessing the growing lack of competency in their new hires, especially from those with a college degree, more and more industries are requiring additional skill certifications and validation testing for aspiring potential job candidates.

Because economic competition is more global than ever, the crisis of competence is more urgent than ever. We must prepare our students to compete, and not merely for university admission and domestic high-paying careers. Unfortunately, an increasing number of countries are outperforming us.

From a global perspective, test scores—specifically ACT scores for our purposes— document a growing number of high school graduates cannot demonstrate competency in core subjects. Measurements of graduates' proficiency in math and science indicate a crisis in our technology-driven world.

Each year, an entire graduating class is less in sync with the way of the future. America's graduates are increasingly less competitive than their counterparts in other developed countries such as China, Korea, and India. American students are lagging behind, and as they go, so goes their nation.

Parents and educators must understand the price of our students' increasing incompetence.

INCOMPETENCE TO BE HIRED

It is also important to point out that a larger issue is emerging today. Our growing incompetence at the primary level is fueling incompetence in secondary and postsecondary institutions. And businesses have noticed. Today, more than ever, companies require potential employees to receive certifications prior to employment. These requirements include softwares such as Microsoft Word and Excel. A job candidate's proficiency in programming languages, writing skills, and reasoning skills are all measured in order to obtain employment, determine compensation, and chart advancement. In addition, more businesses and organizations are tapping international students for employment because they are better educated and prepared for the dictates of the global market.

In 2013, *USA Today* sounded the alarm that American workers' skills lag behind their international counterparts. The PISA in 2018 ranked the US "an unimpressive 38th [https://www.washingtonpost.com/local/education/on-the-world-stage-us-students-fall-behind/2016/12/05/610e1e10-b740-11e6-a677-b608fb-b3aaf6_story.html?utm_term=.e99466bb5b12] out of seventy-one countries in Math and 24th in Science. Among the thirty-five members of the Organization for Economic Cooperation and Development, which sponsors the PISA initiative, the US ranked 30th in Math and 19th in Science." [https://www.usatoday.com/story/news/nation/2013/10/08/literacy-international-workers-education-math-americans/2935909/]

THE HOPE OF COMPETENCE

With costs and losses so great, is there hope that future graduating classes can increase in competence? Indeed there is. In Chapter Three, let's define the competence we want.

CHAPTER 3

WHAT IS COMPETENCE?

You must teach them to your children and talk about them
when you are at home or out for a walk; at bedtime and the
first thing inthe morning.
Deuteronomy 6:7 LVG

Parents are to teach a child morning, noon, and night.
Deuteronomy 6:7, author's paraphrase

Competence is more than academics. Whole competence involves academic ability, a godly character, and leadership skills that include a positive regard for others, and sensitivity.

I define competence as an enduring ability to do something effectively, yielding fruitfulness both qualitatively and quantitatively. Competence consists of demonstrated skills, abilities, and knowledge for a specific field of study.

THE FOUNDATION OF COMPETENCE

Character enables competence. This is especially true in subjects requiring concentration and focus. The competence for study skills is driven by disciplined obedience to a regimen.

Character provides the student the tools to grow their competence.

A person of character honors their parents and family. Discipline and obedience are the promise of fruitfulness; stalwart character enables higher productivity, success, and effectiveness. Academic success results for people of such inward quality.

When someone seeks godliness in their character, they make sacrifices for the good of others. Without complaint, a positive attitude has an equal effect to their caring deeds. A passionate commitment follows God's ways: pursuing equality, justice, and peace for mankind.

A person of godly character is respectful of all persons. Good character seeks the good of others, without regard for race, ethnicity, or creed. Passivity and idleness when injustice can be actively opposed shows a compromised character. As Dr. King said, "A threat to justice anywhere is a threat to justice everywhere." A person of godly character can fulfill his *I Have a Dream* standard, discerning someone's quality not "by the color of their skin but by the content of their character."

(Read "Martin Luther King Jr.'s I Have a Dream' speech in its entirety." *National Public Radio*, January 14, 2022, https://www.npr.org/2010/01/18/122701268/i-have-a-dream-speech-in-its-entirety. Accessed March 11, 2022.)

The measurement of competence discloses the quality of its foundation in character. An honorable character is a critical component of competence. Education can never be limited to possessing knowledge and being able to apply it. Successful education requires students to be equipped with character.

In turn, our graduates keep our culture healthy and thriving. Their well-formed character makes them successful leaders in the marketplace. The Bible says to judge a tree by the fruit that it bears. It is clear, character education cannot be avoided. We dare not consider it less important than math, English, science, and so on.

THE LANGUAGE AND IDENTIFICATION OF CHARACTER

At t.Lab we believe every child should have competency in leadership, technology, finance, and data analysis, with core fundamental skills in English, Math, Reading, and Science. These are common elements of every child's education. A successful education also includes emotional intelligence and leadership.

The use of poor language in America has become rampant, and it is holding us back from excellence. Our leaders, especially those in positions of power, are setting an unattainable example for the rest of us to follow. They may not realize it but their lack of control over their words and limited vocabulary have dire consequences on society.

The Bible tells us that life and death are in the power of the tongue (Proverbs 18:21). But our society tells students that language does not matter. It not only undermines their excellence, but also their competitive character.

The use of poor language is a moral issue too. It shows a lack of respect for oneself and others. It implies that we are willing to accept mediocre standards both in our words and actions. If we want to uphold excellence in the US, we must start by holding ourselves to a higher standard in our language.

Fortunately, there are solutions. Education is one of them. We can teach our children the importance of excellence in their words and actions and encourage them to use respectful language. Another solution is to create stronger incentives for excellence and enforcement of better standards through public policies or incentives. Finally, we must recognize and reward excellence whenever we see it in an effort to create a culture of excellence.

We have the power to create excellence in our language, and the use of poor language can no longer be tolerated. Let us take a stand and make excellence our goal so that we can create a more vibrant, moral, and successful society. By doing this, we can ensure that excellence is seen in all aspects of our lives and future generations. Together, excellence can be ours!

The following table contains the measurable definition of character used by my organization, t.Lab, because the tree of character can be known by these fruits.

1. Honors Parents and Family - Respects and holds parents and family in the highest regard. Constantly seeks insights, opinions, and views on matters germane to life. Looks for opportunities to make parents and family happy and fulfilled.

2. Respects Others, especially Adults - Proactively courteous and polite; maintains order by leveraging the wisdom of others.

3. Disciplined – Focused, well organized, orderly, methodical, and self-controlled while meeting requirements.

4. Obedient – Well trained, dutiful, loyal, self-complaint, follows instruction.

5. Fruitful – Consistently realizes higher levels of productivity, success, and effectiveness in all circumstances and environments.

6. Academic Achievement – Consistently targets, seeks, and realizes higher levels of academic performances.

7. Understands how to compete in an unfair world - Readily identifies and leverages available tools to compete in unjust/biased/unethical environments.

8. Independent Learner – Self-regulating and assumes the responsibility for meeting requirements by educating oneself.

9. Makes Sacrifices – Willfully concedes personal needs/wants for greater need(s) and longer-term value.

10. Thirst and hunger for righteousness – A passionate commitment to following the ways of God by pursuing equality, justice, and peace for mankind while maintaining a positive attitude.

11. Cooperation – Works or acts with another or other persons willingly and agreeably.
12. Competitiveness – Has a strong desire to win or be the best at something and is able to compete successfully with others.

As important as academic competence is, the benefits of character competence are much broader. Effective citizens ensure America leads the frontiers of industry, research and development, and new sciences. By growing students' character, America can lead the world in caring for our fellow man.

> *"I will prepare and someday my chance will come."*
> –Abraham Lincoln

ACADEMIC COMPETENCE AND MEASUREMENT

Academic competence is critical for success in any field. It is crucial to develop competence in a high-demand field or industry.

Of course, there are entrepreneurs and companies that serve society in various capacities that create new products that in turn produce demand for these products. However, the majority of jobs, especially high-paying jobs, are found in industries most in demand: technology, health care, engineering. These fields overlap today more than ever before.

Entrepreneurship is also found in these industries too. The race to produce a COVID vaccine in 2020 and 2021 is an example of overlapping specialties working together to solve a world problem. Today, it is in these fields students must diligently prepare if they are to succeed.

Because academic competence is critical to success in the marketplace, it must be measured. The ACT is one effective tool which gauges competence in core subject areas required of all high school graduates.

Measurement indicates not only knowledge but also the ability to apply it for solutions. To reach identifiable competence, a student must have well-developed reading and writing ability, competence in high school level math, and science skills they are able to apply correctly.

Is the ACT biased, as some say in dismissing it? Yes: it is biased toward academic competence. I've heard all the arguments against standardized tests. Some argue the standardized tests are racially biased; they are not in my opinion. Others maintain the tests fail as a measure of true competence.

To all these I reply, come up with something better then. Until you do, we must be able to measure how students perform. The measurement must reveal their competence both domestically and globally. These tests help do that.

The ACT and other tests like it are biased only in that they reveal what students know and how correctly they can apply that knowledge.

COMPETENCE IN THE KINGDOM ECONOMY

The Lord will make you the head, not the tail. If you pay attention to the commands of the Lord your God that I give you this day and carefully follow them, you will always be at the top, never at the bottom.
Deuteronomy 28:13

Competition is a fundamental element of a market economy, i.e., our American economy. By it, the cost of goods is regulated. Market-share competition within business sectors also drives progress.

Whether individuals compete for employment, or companies compete for market share, competition fuels advancement. When one seeks to gain an edge over others, the competitors respond accordingly. Both among individuals and within industries, self-interest drives man to action in a market economy. It is "a driving power that guides men to whatever work society is willing to pay for," according to Robert Heilbroner, author of *The Worldly Philosophers* when writing about Adam Smith, philosopher, author of *Wealth of Nations*, known as the father of capitalism.

These are true for any market economy; obedient Christians enjoy additional foundational truths. In an economy appropriate to the kingdom of God, in sync with His values and teachings, we expect to be "the head, not the tail" as the Scripture above states.

Where labor is the driving force, Christians should be leaders in every economy, including our own. The more valuable the labor, the higher the compensation. Salaries are higher for careers producing new products or services that have value to provide what others demand.

The Bible verse above, Deuteronomy 28:13, contains more than a promise alone. Once a person becomes a believer, there are performance standards to meet, and when we do, we rise. Walking in integrity, with character and leadership competence, launches our rise to become the head and not the tail.

With this understanding, a child's education should create the competence rooted in faith. Such a student can exhibit character, leadership, academic excellence, and cultural competence. From people with such qualities come the leaders who think critically and apply solutions to real-world problems.

Before any of this can occur, the leaders of tomorrow need the confidence produced by competence.

HUMAN CAPITAL DEVELOPMENT

Dr. Thomas Sowell's definition of human capital development is an important concept for understanding the importance of academic excellence and application mastery in today's world. This definition emphasizes the connection between knowledge, expertise, and wealth, as those with higher levels of education are more likely to create economic prosperity than those without such resources.

Human capital development focuses on the ability to create wealth, which can manifest itself in different ways. This means that having an advanced degree or mastering a particular skill set can lead to increased earnings and better career options. Academic competence and application mastery allow individuals to develop competitive skills for success in the job market and beyond. Furthermore, these competencies are integral for economic growth as those with higher levels of education are more likely to create wealth for their communities.

In conclusion, Dr. Thomas Sowell's definition of human capital development highlights the importance of academic competence and application mastery in economic prosperity. By investing in one's education and mastering a skill set, individuals can achieve that leads to increased incomes and greater competitiveness in the job market. This underscores the need for investing in academic excellence and application mastery, as it is essential for creating wealth and ensuring economic growth.

DEVELOPING COMPETENCE BEGINS AT HOME... BUT NEEDS A VILLAGE

Where does a child begin to understand the value and critical need for Christian identity, irreproachable character, and a first-class education? At home. Deuteronomy 6:7 charges parents to teach their children "morning, noon, and night."

This biblical mandate places the responsibility for each child's education on the parent. This mandate is unchanging. Noah Webster Jr., textbook pioneer—author of Webster's dictionary—said, "Education is useless without the Bible." As a person of faith, I concur. Scripture is clear. The promised blessing of Psalm 112:1–4 is for the parent, and we must not devalue it because the parent is not an educator.

Blessed *is* the man *who* fears the Lord,
Who delights greatly in His commandments.
His descendants will be mighty on earth;
The generation of the upright will be blessed.
Wealth and riches *will be* in his house,
And his righteousness endures forever.
Unto the upright there arises light in the darkness;
He is gracious, and full of compassion, and righteous.

We often hear, "If you don't teach your child, someone else will," and how true this is. The village surrounding the child is teaching them too. If parents do not lead their children firmly, television and others will. While we equate this with wrong behaviors that form character problems, this is true for academics as well. Parents may not teach high-level math or science, but they can and should ensure their children develop competencies in these and other subjects as well. Competencies that ensure future learning is easier, because as we all know, we like to do what we are good at doing. If a child is good at math and science, he or she will enjoy it. Parents must place emphasis on academic competence while continuing to produce the moral foundation, the moral expectations, to help their child choose to live a life of integrity.

Teachers, church, media, entertainment, coaches, every sphere in the village, are influencers in a child's life. Today we have a higher percentage of households lacking the parental knowledge, wisdom, and skills, which disadvantages the young student. Like parents, the child's village must uphold the standard of character and expectation of superior academic performance the parent sets at home.

Teamwork creates success. The onus is not only on the teacher. Educators can attempt to teach character; they can demand that the child develop the discipline for high-level performance. But character is first the job of the parents.

The performance of American students on standardized tests reveals the job is not getting done at large.

HOPE FOR CHARACTER-BASED COMPETENCE

But at my organization, the job is getting done. In cooperation with both parents and t.Lab staff, students are escalating their performance well above the median scores. We are successfully developing human capital one student at a time. Consider the following examples and testimonies.

STUDENT 1: A REAL INCREASE

This female student joined t.Lab in April 2019 as a senior in high school. When she first took the ACT, she scored 21.25. After three months of rigorous work with t.Lab, she increased her practice ACT score to 30.5. When she took the national exam, she scored a composite score of 31!

This raised doubts on her score since she did not get that high on her previous attempt.

t.Lab provided supporting evidence: the resources from t.Lab which enhanced her skills in English, Math, Reading, and Science. With that evidence, she was cleared and her score was finalized.

STUDENT 2: SIGNIFICANT IMPROVEMENT

Student two was an eleventh grade student based in Zahle, Lebanon. Prior to joining t.Lab, he did not know how to operate their printer at home and was not confident in using a computer. One year into the program, he trained and earned nine technology and finance certifications including Word, PowerPoint, Excel, Digital Literacy, Bloomberg Business Market Concepts, and

Artificial Intelligence. He also now knows how to code using Python and helps younger t.Lab students realize technology certifications.

When he joined t.Lab in December 2020, he realized a composite score of 21.5. Since then, he increased his ACT score to 33.

STUDENT 3: QUICK TURNAROUND TO A SCHOLARSHIP

This high school senior had worked for a full tuition scholarship to Michigan State University but her standardized score did not meet the scholarship requirement. After she joined t.Lab in 2021 she increased her score by 8 points in only three months, and qualified for the scholarship grant she wanted.

STUDENT 4: FULL-RIDE SCHOLARSHIP

This young lady joined t.Lab in 2011 as a second grade student. She took her first ACT exam in 2016 and realized a composite score of 18. In 2020, she scored in the 99th percentile (35 out of 36)!

She also became certified in Word, PowerPoint, Excel, and Bloomberg Business Market Concepts. In the summer of 2020, she competed and ranked first in Kettering University's Program for Academically Interested Minds ("AIM") and received a full-tuition scholarship amounting to $258,000.

STUDENT 5: FULL-RIDE SCHOLARSHIP

Student five joined t.Lab in May 2021 as a junior in high school with an ACT score of 26. She realized certifications in Word, PowerPoint, and Excel. In the summer of 2020, she competed in Kettering University's AIM Program. She ranked first in physics with the tutoring and support of Dr. Gilbert Chapman, and ranked fifth overall. In 2022, she got a BorgWarner Scholarship and received a full-ride scholarship with Co-Op to Kettering University amounting to $258,000.

STUDENT 6: FROM LOW TO HIGH, HIGH, HIGH

This young woman has been a participant in t.Lab since 2011 in elementary school. This student is representative of several demographic categories associated with severe academic underperformance within the US. A constant and consistent influence in this student's life hasbeen a strong spiritual connection—as guided by a strong single parent.

This student was a top performer in elementary and middle school. This student faltereda few times after transferring from a much stronger academic Christian high school to an underperforming inner-city school.

The student was provided the opportunity to attend a much-heralded pre-college program in 2019. Upon graduation from high school she entered a top engineering college in Michigan, majoring in bioscience. This student has achieved a 4.0 GPA in her first two semesters. This student has also become certified in MS Suite and Bloomberg Business Market Concepts. The student moved from a low score to 28 on ACT. The student has a perfect 4.0 in one of the toughest majors—simultaneous with a cooperative learning position and a course schedule consisting of nineteen credits or more.

STUDENT 7: DESIRE OF COLLEGES

The story of this t.Lab student showcases the importance of parental engagement and character excellence. Simultaneously it emphasizes the value of mental health in a young person's development.

The student had early access to a strong education foundation that laid the groundwork for the student's future success. However, parental discord arose during the student's middle school to early high school years, and academic performance suffered. It was only when they enrolled in t.Lab that they were able to focus on personal growth and development in a safe environment.

At t.Lab, this student received the support needed, and improved the composite ACT score from 19 to 33—while also taking advantage of educational opportunities like the AIM Pre-College Program. The hard work and dedication of this student resulted in a full-ride scholarship to a major state university, as well as certifications in Microsoft Word, PowerPoint, Excel, and Bloomberg Business Market Concepts.

Ultimately, this student's story exemplifies how investing in the right resources can have a profound impact on the lives of young people. With access to the proper support, guidance, and opportunity, individuals are able to realize their full potential and create a brighter future for themselves. This is precisely what happened with this t.Lab student. Through dedication, hard work, and perseverance, the student was able to overcome both personal and academic obstacles and achieve a level of success.

In stark contrast, we painfully learned from this student that mental health is an essential element of development and success. For academics and competence, it is a story of triumph which proves the power of investing in education. Sadly, it was also a story of despair as the student succumbed to a devastating end-of-life experience.

STUDENT 8: SCIENCE, TECHNOLOGY, ENGINEERING AND MATH (STEM) PREPARATION

The importance of parental involvement in a student's academic and extracurricular success cannot be understated. This is especially true for the case of our t.Lab student, who experienced remarkable achievements both in high school and college. His journey to excellence began with his parents' strong support, which was essential for him to achieve such great heights in STEM-related fields.

Throughout this student's educational career, his parents consistently fostered a learning environment that encouraged excellence and global competitiveness. They provided him with the resources and guidance needed to maximize his potential in both academics and extracurriculars. This support was critical in helping him stay motivated while pursuing challenging courses—such as Physics and Computer Science - that had the potential to open many doors and help him excel at a top-tier college in his chosen field.

The consistent parental involvement throughout our t.Lab student's education was essential for him to achieve his remarkable accomplishments. From helping him develop strong study habits to providing emotional support, the parents' guidance played an integral role in fostering his growth and success. As a result, this student achieved excellence that allowed him to pursue a successful career in STEM fields and demonstrate the importance of parental involvement for academic success—an inspiring reminder of the lasting impact which parental involvement can have on a student's future.

By leveraging their support and guidance, students like our t.Lab student are able to reach their full potential and make a lasting impact on the world. In doing so, we can ensure that no child's success is left behind. With parental involvement, every student has the opportunity to reach their highest level of excellence and make a positive contribution to society through STEM fields or any other avenue.

Parental involvement is an essential part of a student's educational journey, and the story of our t.Lab student serves as a reminder of the importance that it plays in helping students reach their fullest potential. From providing emotional support to fostering a learning environment that encourages excellence and global competitiveness, parents can be integral in setting up their children for long-term success. With the right guidance, any student has the potential to reach remarkable heights, just like our t.Lab student did.

This is a prime example of how parental involvement can help nurture and boost a student's academic and extracurricular achievements. Ultimately, it demonstrates the importance of creating an environment of support and guidance for students in order to help them maximize their potential and achieve excellence. The success of our t.Lab student is a testament to the impact that parental involvement can have on a student's future—and the important role it plays in helping develop an educated, globally competitive society. By leveraging parental involvement, we can ensure that no child's success is left behind.

STUDENT 9: OUR LOGO STUDENT AND FIRST STUDENT TO ATTEND COLLEGE

The story of this t.Lab student is a prime example of what an emotionally mature student and active parental engagement can do to create a high-achieving individual. His commitment to excellence, his global competitiveness, and his willingness to take risks enabled him to reach the top 1 percent of performers in multiple areas.

Throughout college, he used his expansive knowledge and experience to help mentor other students. He was dedicated to helping them raise their ACT scores and become more successful in the classroom. During his time at the London School of Economics, he engaged with some of the most prestigious minds in economics while actively developing his own professional network. The Josiah Institute provided him with an opportunity to gain hands-on experience with a top-tier business curriculum. This student earned the highest honors in his university as both a junior and a senior, Phi Beta Kappa. He set a model we still use today for our students, to plan and prepare for success in college.

In addition to his academic achievements, this t.Lab student used his entrepreneurial spirit to become a successful fast food franchisee and the leader of his own business. His experiences in college provided him with the necessary skills and confidence to be successful in the corporate world.

Through his hard work and dedication, this t.Lab student achieved the highest possible level of success, both academically and professionally. His story serves as an inspiration to students everywhere that it is possible to achieve great things with the right guidance and a strong emotional maturity. Furthermore, it demonstrates the impact that active parental engagement can have on a student's academic and professional aspirations. By providing support, guidance, and encouragement, parents can help their children reach great heights of success.

This t.Lab student is a prime example of what can be achieved with the right mindset and supportive parental involvement. His story serves as an inspiration to students everywhere that excellence is attainable with hard work, dedication, and a strong emotional maturity.

By working together through meaningful dialogue and understanding, parents and students can create an atmosphere of success that leads to growth in both academics and life. This t.Lab student's story is a testament to the power of parent-student collaboration and how it can help young people reach their biggest goals and highest dreams.

The inspiring story of this t.Lab student is a reminder that excellence, ambition, and success are within reach with the right guidance and emotional maturity. With active parental engagement, any student can achieve their goals, no matter how ambitious or lofty they may be. Together, parents and students can create an environment of success and growth.

TESTIMONY 1: SIGNIFICANCE OF COHORTS IN COLLEGE

Attending a major college or university in cohort groups offers numerous benefits to African American students pursuing STEM majors in tier 1 colleges and universities. These benefits include increased academic excellence, competitive advantage, and mental and spiritual support systems.

Academic excellence is one of the most notable advantages that cohort groups provide for any student, including African Americans, who are STEM majors. By pursuing and attending college as a team, African American students have the opportunity to become more deeply invested in both the material being studied and their own academic performance. This deeper investment can lead to higher grades, greater understanding of concepts, and a stronger foundation of knowledge that can be applied to future courses or employment opportunities in their chosen field. The grades matter to indicate mastery and competence.

Furthermore, cohort groups provide students (and especially African American students) a competitive advantage over other STEM majors. Being part of a cohort group allows for deeper and stronger relationships, the sharing of knowledge that can be beneficial when it comes to overcoming obstacles or pursuing entrepreneurial endeavors after college after college. It also provides a sense of family and camaraderie, which can help to foster an environment of collaboration, competition, and trust.

However, the greatest benefit of attending major colleges and universities in cohort groups for African American STEM majors is the mental and spiritual support systems it provides. Being part of a trusted community can be hugely beneficial for students who may feel isolated or alone in their pursuits. It allows them to connect with like-minded individuals with a similar assertiveness to achieve academic goals. Such students represent accountability for each another, not merely in academics but in character and other aspects of successful living. The Bible bears witness that if you are faithful with the interests of someone else, God will be faithful with your interests.

Such accountability partners in a cohort group share similar goals and backgrounds, providing a sense of connection and security. This can create an atmosphere where everyone is working together to help each other achieve their academic goals, making it easier for African American STEM majors to succeed in college and beyond.

Attending a major college or university in cohort groups provides numerous benefits to African American students pursuing STEM majors in tier 1 colleges and universities. By providing increased academic excellence, competitive advantage, and mental and spiritual support systems, cohort groups can be an invaluable resource for African American students in their pursuit of higher education. In short, the advantages of attending a major college or university in cohort groups should not be overlooked. They can help to provide a foundation for success in college and beyond. And that's something to be celebrated.

TESTIMONY 2

The cooperative learning curricula offered at universities such as Kettering University provide a fantastic opportunity for students to develop important skills necessary for success in the modern workplace. Cooperative education occurs when the university places a student in an outside company with a position related to their field of study. The student does work for the company, and the coop student is visible at the CEO level. The expectations and accountability around the student are much higher than other employees, and open doors because of the acute attention given to the student in the company position.

By working in an actual workspace environment, the student gains not only classroom knowledge, but also application mastery. This combination enhances the student's competence and future job and income prospects.

Our students are achieving a mastery at much earlier ages. By working together on projects, students are also able to sharpen their competitive edge while also honing their ability to work with others. This environment of collaboration and teamwork encourages excellence—fostering a sense of comradery and encouraging students to strive for success.

The cooperative learning experience also fosters emotional intelligence, which is an invaluable asset in the professional realm. By having to work closely with others, students must learn how to take the perspectives of their peers into consideration while working toward a common goal. This enables them to become more understanding and empathetic, which are highly sought-after traits in the business world.

While there are clear benefits to participating in cooperative learning curricula, they do come with some challenges as well. Students must learn how to balance their own interests while still working together with others, which can be difficult at times. Additionally, students must also learn how to compromise and work with people who may have different opinions or approaches. Finding success in this environment requires the ability to be flexible and open-minded, something that not all students possess.

In conclusion, cooperative learning curricula offer a great opportunity for students to develop valuable skills necessary for success in the professional world. These curricula challenge students to become more competitive, strive for excellence, and develop emotional intelligence. However, cooperative learning also presents its own unique set of difficulties that must be met in order for each student to find success. By overcoming these challenges, students can gain the skills needed to excel in their college-level studies as well as their future careers.

By participating in cooperative learning curricula, students can become better equipped for the modern workplace and gain invaluable life skills that will prove beneficial far beyond their college experience. This makes cooperative learning an excellent choice for any student looking to get ahead of the competition.

A HERITAGE AND A FUTURE FOR COMPETENCE

The character and competence of our African American forefathers provides a solid foundation and legacy for outstanding academic performance. They have been credited with an important role in creating the strong nation that we know today. Their use of one-room schoolhouses, candlelit homework, and other limited resources to educate their children was a testament to their knowledge, drive, and dedication. The legacy they left behind has been seen throughout history as they won wars, expanded liberty and opportunity, and shaped the world as we know it.

Unfortunately, this legacy is not well-known within the African American community and it must be.

Today, we have many more resources available to us when it comes to educating our students. We have access to modern technology, online classes, and educational materials that were not available in the past. Despite this, why are so many of our students falling behind? One potential reason may be a dearth of changes in educational practices. We need to update how we think and approach education if we are going to prepare our students for success.

Dr. Martin Luther King Jr. once said that "the arc of the moral universe is long, and it bends towards justice" - a statement that can be applied to our current situation. We need to create a culture of excellence in education and strive to instill competence in our students, so they can achieve their full potential. This requires practical solutions that emphasize analytical thinking and critical problem-solving skills. By educating our children with the same dedication and commitment as our forefathers did, we will ensure that justice prevails. Only then will our students have the tools they need to make an impact on their world and shape the future for generations to come.

It is evident that the character and competence of our forefathers were integral to the building of our nation, and critical in allowing us to experience many freedoms and opportunities today. Despite their exemplary efforts, it is no secret that those same liberties have not been afforded to all citizens. This realization has propelled the need for us to become increasingly analytical in our approach to improving educational standards and practices, thereby allowing for a more equitable society.

By updating how we think about education, we can apply practical solutions that will ensure greater excellence in the quality of instruction offered to students. Dr. King's words are poignant—although it may take a long time for justice to be realized, with dedication and commitment we can bend the arc of the moral universe in a way that benefits all. Through our efforts to instill competence in students, we can continue building on the foundations already laid by our forefathers and effect lasting change for generations to come. It is this spirit that will allow us to make history together.

Ultimately, if we are to be successful in maximizing education and opportunity for every citizen, we must create an environment of open-mindedness and growth. With this mindset in place, our students will have the tools necessary to become competent leaders of tomorrow. By taking a proactive stance on educational reform now, we can ensure that the character and competence of our forefathers will serve as an inspiration for a brighter future. By embracing Dr. King's message of justice, we can fight for a more equitable society—one that is based on equality and opportunity for all. And with this, our nation can continue to progress along the rocky road of history. It is up to us to decide if we are going to be the ones that make it happen.

The task of instilling competence in our students is great and requires a multifaceted approach—one that involves analytical thinking, practical solutions, and an emphasis on excellence. By taking a proactive stance towards educational reform now, we can ensure that our nation will continue to be guided by the character and competence of our forefathers—a legacy that will benefit us all. Let us embrace Dr. King's message of justice and create an environment where everyone desires and leverages access to quality education and opportunity– one where we can fight for a more equitable society together. In this way, we can continue to bend the arc of the moral universe towards justice. It is up to us to make it happen.

CHAPTER 4

THE CHANGING PRACTICE OF EDUCATION

Education is not limited to knowledge gained from formal schooling. Knowledge gained in life experience comprises a far greater portion of a person's life. Some people define education as development in the emotional intelligence and empathy necessary for interpersonal relationships.

In our time, education is more broadly defined as the process of developing our intellectual and emotional capacities. This definition considers the development of human potential to be its central aim, with other goals such as truth-seeking or civic engagement not far behind.

Interestingly enough, some people believe that education is a universal right for all children around the world and that it should be available for free in countries like America because it's our responsibility to provide this type of opportunity for all children.

There are also those who argue that our focus needs to shift back towards vocational training, so students can get jobs right out of high school instead of waiting until after college graduation which often leaves them with crippling debt before even beginning their careers.

CLASSIC EDUCATION DEFINITIONS

Throughout time, great men have produced thoughtful, insightful definitions of education. Going back to ancient Greece, Aristotle, who studied under Plato and who became the tutor of Alexander the Great, defined education as "the creation of a sound mind in a sound body." Aristotle believed all men should be educated.

A more recent definition comes from Dr. Martin Luther King Jr. After participating in campus bull sessions at Morehouse College, Dr. King penned a definition of education that encompasses both its function and purpose. In it he expressed concern about students' view of education's purpose. As Dr. King listened to students express their expectation of education, he became concerned that an intellectual-only pursuit, one with the sole intention of succeeding over others, would lead to an absence of morals. Thus, he defined the function of education as a process "to help one think intensively and to think critically," and education's purpose "to create a common set of values that allow us to live together in society." [https://www.washingtonpost.com/news/answer-sheet/wp/2013/01/20/martin-luther-king-intelligence-is-not-enough/]

The goal of a complete education, according to Dr. King, is

> intelligence plus character— that is the goal of true education. The complete education gives one not only power of concentration, but worthy objectives upon which to concentrate. The broad education will, therefore, transmit to one not only the accumulated knowledge of the race but also the accumulated experience of social living.

The function, or job, of education is to help us think intensively and critically. But our purpose—the reason we aspire to higher education—is to further ourselves and our fellow man as well. Dr. King's meaning is that education should espouse our values and lift us and others to new intellectual heights, which in turn advances morals, culture, and commerce. This full definition of education realized fuels and sustains a family's success, which collectively fuels a nation's success.

EDUCATION AND CULTURE

I agree with Dr. King and advance his definition for the issues of our society today—the manifested realization of Dr. King's concerns.

Our past cultural values require a belief in education as respectable and beneficial. Morals of behavior in society must be valued by the majority. Yet, in today's majority culture, such firmly held values seem to have fallen by the wayside.

Compare the influence of churches in Dr. King's time with the influencers of today. Where he and his generation fought with blood, sweat, tears and life, today's greatest influencers are on social media. As measured by followers, the top fifty are celebrities, musicians, and sports figures. [https://www.visualcapitalist.com/worlds-top-50-influencers-across-social-media-platforms/] Compare the number of their followers with the pastors, teachers, and others who transmit cultural values such as morality. It does not bode well for our society and must urgently be rebalanced.

Celebrity, and not the hard work of celebrities, is the primary reason why people follow famous people. Most people don't expect a relationship with these influencers, nor seek to mimic their work ethic, regimen, and character.

THE T.LAB DEFINITION

It is the value of morality that must resurface in culture and society, and even inside the church. Morality must be deployed and displayed by all leaders. At t.Lab, we agree: education must present and transmit our values and firmly held beliefs. Our definition of education is a descriptive one, addressing both process and purpose:

> Education is the systematic process of giving and receiving targeted information to realize a measured goal or vision. Education enables information to be converted into human capital as knowledge, skills, habits, competencies, and wisdom. The competence of education determines the return that society realizes from their citizens, human capital, and human resources.

We believe that education is a process that exists for the purpose of giving and receiving information to reach a goal or vision. Notice the process of both giving and receiving. In early grades the giving is generally from the teacher. As a student matures, a classroom should be increasingly competitive. Students should arrive not only prepared but ready to communicate their knowledge and thoughts to other students. Competitive classrooms create exponential learning because application of learned material is expected, and the myriad views offered create a broad worldview that fuels learning.

If education, influenced by the other mountains of society, is the primary driver of student success, then what drives education? Think about this for a moment. The top influencers driving education today are technology with significant shifts in standards for culture, industry, and performance.

FORCES OF CHANGE: COVID-19

There is no doubt about it. COVID forced changes in every sphere of society: education, family, industry, media, entertainment, and government. Practically everything in our lives changed because of the recent pandemic.

Recognizing our growing incompetence, we must also acknowledge educational change forced by COVID-19 and other pathogenic influences. Such risks to educational success are an ongoing concern. Such threats will repeat or may even be on the horizon.

To address our growing incompetence, a critical discussion must define a path forward. Both this discussion and the solutions achieved must address the crisis of competence in education. Our pro3blems did not begin with COVID, which highlighted them and forced us to consider changes. If our response results in a push toward achieving student competence, we will pass the test. Our students will come out more competent rather than less.

Where and how we educate has changed for the majority of American students. Where and how we work, shop, socialize... the major features of life have changed to a large degree as well.

EXAMPLE: INCREASED COMPETENCE FORCED BY COVID

Dr. Michael Crow's decisive and forward-thinking leadership has enabled Arizona State University to develop digital solutions that have prepared the university for the challenges posed by Covid-19 before the pandemic even broke out. Through his guidance, ASU has leveraged information technology to empower its students and faculty with digital transformation and competency while also ensuring global competitiveness.

Dr. Crow's digital revolution has enabled ASU to move away from traditional methods of learning and work and embrace digital solutions. He recognized the need to implement digital transformation before the pandemic, allowing the university to be better prepared compared to many other universities who were caught off guard by Covid-19 and had no digital infrastructure in place. The digital transformation has included the implementation of digital learning and work platforms, new digital tools such as AI, data analytics and cloud computing, as well as virtual meetings, lectures, and conferences.

In addition to implementing digital solutions, Dr. Crow also saw the need for students and staff to be digitally competent so that they could take full advantage of digital solutions. As such, he has worked closely with the university's digital team to develop digital competency plans for both students and staff comprising of digital learning opportunities and digital literacy programs. He also established collaborations between ASU and other global universities to ensure that its students are at par with their peers in other parts of the world when it comes to digital competency and global competitiveness.

Dr. Crow's digital initiatives have proven to be instrumental in helping ASU prepare for the challenges of Covid-19 before the pandemic even broke out, and these digital solutions have enabled students and staff to realize excellence throughout the university despite the challenges posed by the pandemic. His digital vision has enabled ASU to be one of the most digital-ready universities in the nation, allowing it to thrive and remain competitive during this difficult time.

In conclusion, Dr. Michael Crow's digital leadership has been instrumental in preparing Arizona State University for the challenges of Covid-19 before the pandemic. Through his guidance, the university has leveraged digital transformation and digital competency to ensure global competitiveness, digital readiness and student excellence. His digital initiatives have proven invaluable in allowing ASU to cope with the difficult times of the pandemic and beyond.

FORCES OF CHANGE: CULTURAL SHIFTS
Pre-COVID, America's education delivery was rooted in our existence as an agricultural society. Standards for the traditional classroom were developed when such a populace was the majority. No

wonder that traditional classroom is facing so many challenges producing competence in students.

The world is evolving at a rapid pace, and education has to adapt. For example, cultural isolation is less possible than ever. Long gone are the days when students' only influencers were those of the same culture, and curriculum concerned itself with only the majority culture. In the last few decades, multiculturalism has become prevalent in many different parts of the world.

This is showcased in education. Now students must work with people from different cultures and backgrounds. Curriculum in schools today is more inclusive and culturally sensitive, to accommodate more cultures within a school system. For example, there are more languages being taught and spoken in classrooms.

Multiculturalism also influences how students are grouped together in certain class subjects, such as math. Students from different cultures are mixed together to learn from one another as well as broaden their perspectives on topics.

Educators are also trying to make education more inclusive by teaching students about the cultures of different countries and how they influence society. One way this is accomplished is through history lessons, where multiculturalism can be seen in various time periods throughout the world.

Educators are now teaching students faced with different cultural backgrounds. The students' future work will include work with people of different cultures. The ability to work with people from different cultures, backgrounds, and languages is a competency that education must produce, and should be taught at a young age—becoming second nature for our students.

FORCES OF CHANGE: INDUSTRY SHIFTS

Education has always had to adapt. Otherwise, it would be outdated. Now more than ever, education needs to be flexible and responsive as industries undergo the most significant transformations they have seen since the industrial revolution.

Industry and education have been closely associated since the industrial revolution. In fact, during this time period, a shift began from an agricultural economy to a manufacturing one. Workers were employed based on how well they could do their jobs—as determined by teachers and employers. Schools were needed to educate new workers for these industries. Education evolved out of the churches as a ministry, both to students and to society.

The industrial revolution brought many changes to the workforce. For example, more people worked outside of the home and women began entering the workforce in larger numbers. This created a need for different teaching methods that were able to accommodate a wider range of learning styles.

The first educational professionals were teachers who taught at schools established by industry owners. These schools were set up to help students learn the skills needed for their jobs in industry. Students learned how to use machinery and perform their tasks in a way that optimized production. Teachers trained students based on what they knew was required of them by employers.

Those who did not have access to formal education worked with apprenticeships, where it was assumed that employees learned their job from on-the-job training. During World War II, factory owners began to prefer highly educated workers with specialized skills. In response, more schools were established for children of working families and more adults began attending night school.

The automotive industry has always been a leader in education reform. Ford Motor Company started a training school in 1916 and launched many innovative programs for workers. They offered courses to prepare workers for new jobs and paid them while they learned. Universities established engineering departments that helped workers become qualified to work with new machinery.

During the industrial revolution, the need for many jobs increased. This created a pressing demand for education to train students in job skills. While there were many schools that taught basic academic subjects, these did not adequately prepare students for their future jobs.

And so, industries began establishing their own training programs and hiring or firing based on performance. For example, Ford Motor Company's "Chautauqua Assembly" program taught workers how to use complex machinery by putting them through a training session where they had to fix one of the machines. In addition, many companies hired experienced workers and apprentices with whom they worked closely. These apprenticeships offered on-the-job training that allowed employees to learn to do their jobs over time.

In the late nineteenth century, night schools for adults became more popular. These schools opened many opportunities to people who needed education in order to work at new jobs. For example, David Lubin founded the International Correspondence Schools ("ICS") of Scranton, Pennsylvania. This organization made it possible for students to learn from home by sending instructional materials and teachers to the student's doorstep. ICS was created because David Lubin saw that new immigrants needed an education in order to get jobs in newly developed industries but could not afford school.

During World War II, many people did not have access to work experience since so many men were fighting in the war. In response, industrialists created a gamut of training programs to help unqualified workers learn what they needed to know to do their jobs. Many industries started up schools that taught new skills and provided on-the-job training where trainees took turns doing different tasks. The goal was to get people hired as quickly as possible so that factory owners could meet the demand for workers during this time.

The need for more education led to changes in how it was delivered. "Twelve-year schools" were founded, which meant smaller groups of students went through more rigorous instruction at a faster pace. This allowed each student to learn more in a shorter period of time. Many schools also began providing more one-on-one instruction, which helped students better understand what was being taught.

Industrialists played an important role in the development and delivery of education for factory workers. Their influence was both direct on schools and indirect through their own training programs. In recent years, the role of industry in education has shifted as government programs have taken over much of the responsibility for educating people.

Now that America is no longer an agricultural or manufacturing driven economy, education must prepare students to lead at home and globally both now and into the future.

EDUCATION FOR AN INFORMATION-DRIVEN SOCIETY

Senator Lamar Alexander (R-TN) served in numerous positions of educational leadership. After eight years as Tennessee governor, he served as president of the University of Tennessee system, followed by service as the Secretary of Education and finally his election to the United States Senate in 2003.

With these qualifications, his 2013 address to the Tennessee Higher Education Commission in Nashville knowledgeably defines the change forced upon educators. Redefining college success for the twenty-first century, the senator says that the United States is now an "industry driven economy," and higher education has to recognize that.

Alexander said that fewer than one in thirty students graduate from college with a major or minor in engineering. He referred to the US education system as "a system of preparing people for jobs that either no longer exist or will soon disappear." The senator believes that countries like China have an edge in industry because they are focused on education to achieve goals in today's economy.

Senator Alexander said that the same effort should be made here in America. Similarly, Governor Bill Haslam told the board members that success in their state is tied to improving education and reducing the dropout rate.

Education in America should focus more on real-world applications of industry knowledge as well as a global outlook. While many developed countries rely on strong economies to maintain their status, the United States has become an economy driven by technology which requires skilled labor both here and abroad. Education is the gateway to keeping America strong as an economic superpower into this century.

Alexander feels that it is necessary to restructure higher education in order for students to be ready in today's highly competitive work force: "Our education system must prepare people for jobs that are open now, not just those of thirty years ago."

FORCES OF CHANGE: COMPETITIVENESS

One of the most important tasks for our nation is to ensure that it remains secure. In order to do this, we must maintain a strong and well-educated population. This is why the US Council on Competitiveness has dedicated itself to the cause of promoting educational policies in the United States that will help create an educated workforce capable of tackling the challenges of the future.

The Council on Competitiveness believes that the current education system in the United States is inadequate and fails to meet the demands of a competitive global economy. The lack of educational opportunity, resources, and quality instruction contributes to a sense of national insecurity that could have serious consequences for our nation's security. This sentiment has been echoed by the Department of Defense, which noted in 2018 that "an inadequate and under-resourced educational system increases the risks to national security."

The Council on Competitiveness promotes initiatives that focus on improving access to quality education, developing cutting edge research, and creating tools for employers to create a well-educated workforce. All of these efforts are aimed at helping ensure the United States remains a powerhouse in the world economy, and more importantly, that it is safe from security threats. Through these initiatives, the council hopes to give America's youth the opportunity to become informed citizens and empowered members of society.

By promoting educational reforms, investing in research programs and creating tools for employers to better assess the skills of potential employees, the US Council on Competitiveness is working towards ensuring that our nation remains safe and competitive in an ever-changing global landscape. The council believes that investing in education will lead to stronger national security and a more prosperous future for all Americans. It is only through the commitment to these initiatives that we can make sure our nation remains safe and prosperous for generations to come.

As the US Council on Competitiveness noted, "Our shared mission is to ensure that America's global competitiveness and national security are maintained by promoting excellence in education. We must continue to invest in our children's future and ensure that they are given the resources and opportunities to succeed." Investing in education is investing in our nation's security. The US Council on Competitiveness seeks to ensure that America remains strong and secure, both now and into the future.

The US Council on Competitiveness is committed to creating a better future for all Americans and protecting our nation from security threats. By investing in education and creating opportunities for our youth, we can ensure that the United States remains strong and competitive on a global scale. Together, we can make sure that America continues to be a leader in innovation and technology, while also providing its citizens with an education system fit for the future.

EDUCATION RECONSTRUCTION FOR AMERICA

The following ideas are proposed for consideration toward facilitating a restructuring of higher education in America.

First, students today will find the highest-paying jobs in technology, IT-related fields, science, and healthcare-based fields. We are on the precipice of shifting from oil and gas to solar, wind, and other forms of renewable energy, for example. We are in a race with China to land on Mars first. Surgeries once only performed by skilled surgeons are now performed robotically. The knowledge of technology combined with medical knowledge is healing and improving the quality and longevity of life for many.

These are the industries that are shaping and improving life now and the industries that will need qualified, competent employees well into the future. Knowing this, each sector alongside parents and educators must prepare our students for today's jobs while simultaneously inspiring students to understand today's problems so they can aspire to create tomorrow's solutions. To do this, our entire village must work together, education with parents, business, media, arts and entertainment, government, and church.

To maintain our position as a global leader in these areas we must innovate, stay ahead of the competition while creating allies throughout the world with like-minded and governed countries. Our students must be ready to step into high-value technical, medical, and scientific roles.

We cannot remain stagnant. We must adapt quickly to keep up with change, to keep up with industry shifts, anticipating them, so our students can anticipate future problems and develop the solutions necessary. Technology as a driver of education can help us achieve this.

Should we be responding to industry shifts or anticipating and creating new innovations and paradigms? At one time universities drove innovation—I wonder why? Has it been impacted by the commercialization of college education?

GM: SALARY BUYOUTS

The recent announcement by General Motors that it is offering buyouts to a majority of its salaried workforce has far-reaching implications for college students and those in the secondary level of education. It is an alarming reminder that digital competencies are essential for competitiveness in the global market, and digital technologies will play an increasingly important role in determining global dominance.

For college students, this means having the digital skills to stay ahead of the curve. They need to be equipped with digital competencies such as coding, robotic process automation (RPA), artificial intelligence (AI), and analytics to remain competitive in their chosen field. The demand for digital professionals has also increased significantly, with organizations looking for employees who have strong technical backgrounds, including experience in software engineering or digital marketing.

For secondary school students, the focus should be on digital literacy and understanding how digital technologies are impacting their world. Schools should invest in digital learning strategies that empower young people to develop their digital skills and become more digitally responsible citizens. This includes not only teaching digital competencies but also helping students understand the implications of digital technology on their lives and the world around them.

These changes show that digital competency is no longer a "nice-to-have" skill; it is an essential requirement for any student hoping to remain competitive in today's job market. Therefore, it is critical for college students and those in secondary level education to embrace these changes and prioritize developing their digital skills if they want to be successful in the digital age.

This article was written to provide insight into the implications of the recent announcement by General Motors regarding salary buyouts of a majority of its salaried workforce and its impact and implications for college students and those in secondary level of education. It highlights digital competencies as an essential requirement for competitiveness in the global market, and outlines steps that students should take to remain competitive in today's digital age. Ultimately, it is critical for college students and those in secondary level education to prioritize developing their digital skills if they want to be successful in the digital world.

EXAMPLE: INCREASED COMPETENCE FORCED BY INDUSTRY CHANGES

Mary Barra is a leader with an unwavering commitment to excellence. After graduating from General Motors Institute (Kettering University) with a degree in Mechanical Engineering, she continued her career at General Motors, the global automotive leader. While at General Motors, she pursued and completed the Master's Degree in Mechanical Engineering from Stanford University. She rotated through a variety of assignments, each with increasing responsibility and scope. As CEO of GM, she has been able to drive change through digital transformation and innovative initiatives that have helped make it one of the most successful companies worldwide. Her success is a testament to her leadership capability and readiness for global markets.

Mary Barra is a model for diversity, inclusion, and change in the corporate world. Through her focus on hiring competent and diverse talent from across the globe, she is creating a culture that drives innovation, change, and outstanding business results (competence). She has also taken bold steps to push for greater representation in the boardroom and executive offices. She is a model for aspiring leaders who are seeking an edge in the global marketplace.

Mary Barra has been able to successfully bring GM into the century, through her focus on digital transformation, technological advancements, and green initiatives. Her leadership has ultimately transformed General Motors into a leading technology corporation and industry leader. Through her determination and ambition to continuously push for progress, Barra is an example of what can be achieved when excellence is pursued ardently. She stands as a beacon of success in the corporate world, reminding all aspiring leaders that true achievement comes with competence, hard work, focus, and dedication. Mary Barra is a shining example of excellence and global leadership.

FORCES OF CHANGE: ACADEMIC PERFORMANCE SHIFTS

Shifting standards for academic performance are also forcing change to educational practices. A recent report from the National Center for Education Statistics found that "overall college enrollment rates are projected to decline by 18% between 2020-2025." This will lead to a job market in which people who have two-year degrees or certificates may not be able to find jobs in their desired profession because there will be too many people with similar qualifications.

One of the major factors that contributes to this problem is a moving goal line for what's considered "college-ready," and it influences the types of courses that are offered to students. For example, in the past, a student would be considered ready for college if they took math and science classes through their junior year of high school. Nowadays, it's not uncommon for schools to require these same students to take advanced algebra or calculus coursework before graduation from high school.

There's also the issue of balancing what is considered "academic rigor" and ensuring that students are provided with opportunities to explore their interests. For example, the state of California has been criticized for lack of breadth in its curriculum. Critics decry how it missed opportunities to explore topics outside of STEM.

The most popular courses offered during this time were related to mathematics and science because they provide students with the opportunity to earn college credits while still in high school. But STEM topics are crucial for every student to explore, and even for those who want to avoid STEM fields later in life. Many people consider this a terrible problem because it can lead to students not having the opportunity to explore their interests outside of what are considered "acceptable" degrees. But there is also concern that too much focus on non-STEM topics could be detrimental as well because it would be taking away from the much-needed focus on STEM fields.

NEW THINKING

Moving ahead, then, we must determine how we can leverage these changes to create success and advancement in education that will turn the tide on our decreasing competence.

As we look at the countries performing higher academically than America, we first must accept that we need to tackle our issue of decreasing competence. This includes our incompetence in education, as evidenced by test scores, as well as our decreasing levels of leadership competence, and cultural competence, which was brought to light in our country's recent racial issues and through ACT scores for minority students including African Americans.

"A rising tide raises all boats," said John F. Kennedy. And rising competence will impact every sector of society. Our culture will shift when education integrates character and competence. Fewer protests and riots will result from more academic collaboration and competition which forces our families and students to grow. Instead of defaulting to culture's influence on our young, we can train them in doing the right thing. More shepherds after God's heart can lead students into right lifestyles and successful careers.

To change the tide, however, we will require a paradigm shift. One that will flow from and into every sphere of society forming a culture shift, a shift that values and aids the education mountain, which is the primary driver of continued success for our nation.

To turn the tide to rising competence, a paradigm shift, a village paradigm that promotes whole competence, must occur *now*. Educators, educational leaders, and key stakeholders are the leaders of this needed paradigm shift, as they must do their part by continuing and furthering a technology-driven education delivery.

NEW TOOLS

With the ability of technology to individualize learning, printed textbooks, pens and pencils are becoming a hinderance in classrooms. Classrooms and teachers, however, will remain critical.

This needed shift was never clearer to me than when I dropped by a small, suburban library to pick up books to include in our book drive, "50,000 books for Africa." This library was giving away thousands of books, books they paid money for. I began to wonder if people really read the books, if there was truly a return on investment. A technology-driven curriculum is certainly necessary now, and as a driver of education it has benefits that books, pens or pencils, and paper just do not have.

Technology offers individualized learning both in a classroom setting and at home. By using technology-driven curriculum, teachers can monitor each student's progress and step in to help when needed. Technology offers individualization without a teacher spending hours accessing each student's progress. The information collected through the software or curriculum delivery system is immediately available to the teacher, which provides real-time valuable information about the student's progress. Technology is helping students develop competence incrementally and can help eliminate gaps in knowledge in a specific subject.

This is the major shift upon us. We must imagine an environment that maximizes productivity and output. We are at the forefront of utilizing technology in greater ways. Our schools are at the forefront of relying on technology to deliver curriculum.

Technology also offers greater opportunity to cultural exchanges. Students in a technology-driven learning environment can easily work alongside students from other countries. Through cultural interactions, students grow in cultural competence. They learn from one another and grow worldviews.

Technology should deliver curriculum in conjunction with a teacher in the classroom. Technology can aid teachers and students in ways that can allow both to excel in their roles. Let's imagine and produce a future where education focuses on students and their competence uppermost.

The takeaway is that technology that provides digital learning, online curriculum delivery, will become the primary driver of education in the future. Indeed, the past decade has been a revolutionary one for education. In the last ten years, we have seen the growth of Massive Open Online Courses ("MOOCs") through organizations like edX and Coursera, which allow students to learn from world-class universities without paying tuition or even being on campus. We've seen an increase in flipped classrooms, where teachers use technology to deliver lectures online while in-person classroom time is used for collaborative work between teacher and student. And with new mobile devices entering into our lives at breakneck speed (most notably tablets), we are seeing how this technology can transform learning by providing interactive textbooks that provide instant feedback to test questions and real-time data about how students are performing in class. There is a need to identify the right metrics in education. These changes will undoubtedly affect how future generations learn both inside and outside the classroom, but for now they remain largely in the realm of possibility.

HARKNESS METHOD

The Harkness Method has proven to be an effective tool for producing excellence in independent learning among secondary level students. By allowing students the competitive and cooperative exchanges of ideas and perspectives, the Harkness Method encourages critical thinking and develops independent learners with the skills necessary to succeed in a rapidly changing world. The collaborative nature of the Harkness Method helps students to recognize the importance of teamwork and collaboration in order to achieve excellence. It also encourages students to take ownership of their education, allowing them to develop the essential skills needed for independent learning.

The Harkness Method is an innovative approach that has been proven successful in preparing secondary level students for college and beyond. This method effectively cultivates independent learners with the skills to thrive in a rapidly changing and competitive environment. It encourages critical thinking, develops teamwork and collaboration, and allows students the opportunity to take ownership of their education. For excellence in independent learning at the secondary level, the Harkness Method is an invaluable tool for educators.

This excellence in independent learning can help students to become successful in college and beyond—giving them a solid foundation that will prepare them for life after graduation. With the Harkness Method, excellence in independent learning at the secondary level is achievable.

https://www.harknessmethod.org/about-the-method/what-is-the-harkness-method/

https://www.harknessmethod.org/wp-content/uploads/2020/03/Harkness-Method-Booklet_2.pdf

https://www.nea.org/tools/59715.htm

https://erlangerllc.com/harkness-method/

http://edtechreview.in/news/1722-the-influence-of-collaborative-learning

CLASSROOM LEADERSHIP USING THE PERFORMANCE SCORECARD

To promote classroom leadership, an education development process can be implemented. At t.Lab, students are required to develop detailed study plans two months before the new semester begins. By having their clear plan in place, students can prepare for their classes and be ready to respond to any surprises during the course of the semester. And the plan functions as the student's personal scorecard because its measurable elements enable self-evaluation.

This method encourages students to think about their academic goals for the semester. The student creates achievable strategies for reaching them. But the benefits expand beyond the individual student.

The development planning process and performance scorecard also sets the tone for a productive classroom environment. Each student has one and becomes responsible for his or her own individual preparation. Their own development plan adds self-motivated personal accountability. Such students arrive on time, submit homework on time, ask and answer questions, take meaningful notes, build consensus on key topics, volunteer assistance, and submit articles for classroom consumption.

Day by day, the student uses the scorecard to measure their level and participation in the class. It is a distinct process where a student must develop a detailed learning plan for the class. In their own plan, they can identify the diligence and actions to succeed in the class: turning in homework, being on time, answering questions on tests. At t.Lab, our students each have an educational development plan with ten distinct standards for each class, each day.

When a student's performance can be measured by these particular factors, a sense of responsibility is cultivated within the entire classroom setting. Students who are more prepared can actively participate in the learning process. The classroom environment becomes conducive to meaningful discussions and promotes the development of leadership skills among students.

Ultimately, both students and instructors benefit significantly. This education development process gives each student their own performance scorecards. A culture of preparation and responsibility takes root in the classroom. Not only does this method help ensure that each student is adequately prepared for class, but it also enables students to build leadership skills, applicable far beyond their academic studies.

By incorporating an education development process into the classroom, we can ensure that students are better prepared for coursework, can exhibit increased levels of classroom leadership, and can build important skills that will stay with them far beyond their academic years.

INDEPENDENT LEARNING MATERIAL

At any level of education, producing students who are independent learners is paramount. Such students can leverage time management skills and develop classroom leadership. When students have these abilities, they can become competitive in their fields, working towards global excellence and creating a more competitive environment. Through this independence and understanding of how to effectively manage their time, they can pursue higher goals without the help of external support. This encourages students to become more self-sufficient and confident in their chosen field, boosting performance. Furthermore, those who have strong leadership skills can create a positive atmosphere within the classroom, making it easier for group projects or activities to complete tasks on time.

Additionally, fostering resourceful and independent learners at the secondary level is advantageous for the long-term. Students can become better prepared to enter college or the workforce, understanding how to take charge and complete their tasks successfully. This allows them to hit the ground running when it comes to more complex assignments and projects that may require advanced problem-solving skills. Furthermore, as a result of gaining valuable experience in self-management and classroom leadership, students can become more proactive in their academic career, setting themselves up for success.

In conclusion, producing students who are independent learners at the secondary level of education is essential in fostering a future of global excellence. By encouraging them to gain experience in time management skills and classroom leadership principles, these students can become better equipped to take charge of their academic careers and become more competitive in their fields. With this understanding, they can develop the confidence necessary to pursue higher goals and create a more competent environment.

By investing in students at the secondary level, we can equip them with the skills needed to become successful independent learners, paving the way towards global excellence.

STUDENT EXPECTATIONS

What do students think about these new opportunities? Are they eager to take advantage of them? Will we see a wave of impatient change agents among our students who champion this brave new world more than their teachers and administrators? Unfortunately, it doesn't look like it.

According to the results of a survey by Education First, a group that does research on international education, only 34% of students agree with the statement, "I'm excited about new advances in technology at school." This percentage is significantly lower than the 52% who are excited about IT opportunities outside of school. Given that these surveys were generally given to high school-age students, this finding is particularly troubling. While we expect these opinions to shift as these students enter college and discover the many benefits that technology can provide for learning, it's clear that there are a lot of students who aren't interested in taking advantage of the educational opportunities available to them.

Another 37% of students disagree with this statement while only 27% agree, leaving us with only 32% of students who are excited about the educational innovations that could make their education more effective and enjoyable. But this result is actually worse than it seems at first glance. The percentages show that there is far less excitement among female students (28%) than male ones (39%).

This disparity may be explained by "boys will be boys" thinking, which would predict that male students are more likely to pursue new technologies because they want to stay competitive in the labor market. Or it may be explained by gendered myths about girls' abilities, which would predict less enthusiasm among girls for new technology-enabled learning strategies. To draw any real conclusions, we need to dive into the data and ask our female students what they think about these changes, and we need to make sure those voices are heard.

The Education First survey also broke down excitement for new technology by different regions of the world. Interestingly, students from East Asia (not including Japan) were most excited about technological innovations in education at 48%, while students from Western Europe were least excited at only 24%. Students in Latin America (35%) and Africa (38%) fell somewhere in the middle. The region that was most excited about IT innovations outside of school, however, was Latin America at a whopping 58%.

This is unsurprising given recent trends to "gamify" education by using contemporary gaming technologies. While this gamification may seem like a passing fad, it may wind up having the greatest potential for permanently transforming education because it is so inherently motivating. Students are naturally drawn to competitive games and activities that encourage them to learn and "win." Deeper learning experiences are simply an added benefit.

TEACHER EXPECTATIONS

While students have some doubts about how useful technology will be in their lives, teachers are a lot more enthusiastic. The Education First survey found that 62% of teachers agree that their students will be better prepared to enter the workforce when they fully and effectively use technology in school, but only 23% of teachers believe that students are currently being well- prepared for the future workplace.

This lack of preparation is especially pronounced among secondary teachers, who think that only 20% of their students are adequately prepared for the workforce. The majority (71%) believe that many students will need to go back to school once they enter the workforce and employers realize how little technology-savvy they actually are.

Teachers' enthusiasm for technological innovation is matched on an international level as well, according to the Education First survey. The percentages of teachers who believe that their students will be better prepared for the workplace when they fully use technology in school range from 52% in Western Europe to 85% in East Asia (not including Japan).

Teachers in Latin America were particularly enthusiastic at 84%, but given recent educational reforms that prioritize technological literacy for Latin American students, this is hardly surprising. Compared to their peers who teach at the university level, secondary teachers are much more concerned about how technology will make them more competitive on-the-job market in terms of acquiring new skills and meeting unfamiliar challenges—concerns that may be even greater among primary school teachers.

To align our future with the deployment models of the past is a mistake. Teachers cannot be the sole source of knowledge as they once were. We must design and deploy systems that provide scale, scope, and productive capability in students. Technology must be utilized for educational purposes.

Student-created content (video, audio, etc.) can be uploaded to the World Wide Web for assessment and peer review. Students can work together in virtual teams to complete a given task. Digital tools can provide distance learning opportunities between students and teachers. The possibilities are endless, but their effectiveness will largely depend on how they are implemented and what is expected of the students.

Using technology to help students keep up with industry needs and shifts also empowers our students to know and better understand tomorrow's problems now. Potentially, this develops interest that a teacher can encourage. Technology, when used correctly, makes teaching easier. Now is not the time to eliminate the benefits COVID began. It is time to merge the best of technology with the classroom. This will require more than teachers delivering the same curriculum over a video-based classroom. This performance shift teachers must embrace will incorporate technology as the driver of student learning.

From my vantage point as an adjunct professor and t-Lab founder, I know it is crucial for us to respond to the current influencers of education by embracing them now. We must allow these influencers to do their job—drive education—to force our growth, further competence, and elevate our students to the forefront of industry. While teachers should know and understand marketplace shifts and changes, they cannot know everything. Technology, however, can easily provide current industry or research information, and can keep students inspired and learning current, leading curriculum that can fuel individual progress.

EDUCATION NOW

At the secondary level of education, producing students who are independent learners and leverage time management skills and classroom leadership principles is paramount. When students have these abilities, they can become competitive in their fields, working towards global excellence and creating a more competent environment. Through this independence and understanding of how to effectively manage their time, they can pursue higher goals without the help of external support. This encourages students to become more self-sufficient and confident in their chosen field, boosting performance. Furthermore, those who have strong leadership skills can create a positive atmosphere within the classroom, making it easier for group projects or activities to complete tasks on time.

Additionally, fostering resourceful and independent learners at the secondary level is advantageous for the long-term. Students can become better prepared to enter college or the workforce, understanding how to take charge and complete their tasks successfully. This allows them to hit the ground running when it comes to more complex assignments and projects that may require advanced problem-solving skills. Furthermore, as a result of gaining valuable experience in self-management and classroom leadership, students can become more proactive in their academic career, setting themselves up for success.

In conclusion, producing students who are independent learners at the secondary level of education is essential in fostering a future of global excellence. By encouraging them to gain experience in time management skills and classroom leadership principles, these students can become better equipped to take charge of their academic careers and become more competitive in their fields. With this understanding, they can develop the confidence necessary to pursue higher goals and create a more competent environment.

By investing in students at the secondary level, we can equip them with the skills needed to become successful independent learners, paving the way towards global excellence.

Teachers also have to keep up with the changing world and how it is affecting education. They need to be aware of what changes are happening in society so that they can help students understand these developments, as well as stay informed about current events like climate change or immigration laws.

This all starts at home; if parents don't want their children to grow up in a world of intolerance, they need to teach them tolerance and acceptance. Children are sponges; if parents talk about the importance of multiculturalism at home, their children will learn it better than they would from someone else later on down the line.

In addition to adjusting education for future social demographics and a future job market, we must seek to produce competent students who are godly leaders, a goal that is well worth the journey. Old paradigms must change. A new way of thinking must emerge. Old paradigms rooted in the traditional classroom with books and pens must change. Instead, current paradigms that embrace technology as an important part of the classroom are critically necessary.

Current paradigms that encourage parents to allow media, entertainment, and friends to influence a student to a greater degree than parents must change. A growing paradigm that faith and church are no longer important to a family's life must change. By changing these paradigms, competence increases, communities change, and culture also changes.

When we embrace and form godly character, godly leadership, and educational competence as our goals and put the work in to ensure our students reach this whole competence, culture itself will change to reflect who we are and who we want to be.

Performance shifts need to be addressed within each sphere in our village. From leaders of businesses to religious, entertainment, and media leaders, every sphere has a role and interest in ensuring we develop student competence now. If our students win, America wins.

Dr. King said, the two most dangerous things on the planet are sincere ignorance and conscious stupidity. Today I see many people, including many of our leaders, offering solutions that are not solutions. Some of these leaders perhaps do not realize the old ways or hasty solutions will no longer work—sincere ignorance. Then there are those in academia who go along even when they do not believe the solution is actually a solution simply because it is expedient or personally beneficial to do so; this is conscious stupidity.

For example, I do not agree with forgiving college loan debt. College loan debt can be an investment if a diligent, competent student has a clear plan for the future that is fostered and nourished by their village. Cost implies value after all, so free is easy. College should never be considered to be easily obtained, nor should it simply become a check mark on the path to whatever career a person wants. College is an investment of time and money. The cost ensures the student sees it as an investment. A diligent student will invest the time and energy in primary school required to receive college acceptances, potential scholarships, and so on. Competence should be our goal. College represents opportunity. College is not a right for all students, if not earned. Competition is a reality in our lives: domestic competition and global competition. And competition is not going away. We must prepare our children. Every sphere of society, our entire village is needed to raise the tide, and neither sincere ignorance nor conscious stupidity can be allowed.

It is time to face the reality of our decreasing competence while remaining encouraged by our students' unlimited potential. No, this is not an easy road. The outcome, the gain—student competence—is well worth the effort. Every sphere of our society will be affected.

CHAPTER 5

SEVEN MOUNTAINS WHERE EDUCATION MEETS COMPETENCE

America still has the greatest capacity of any nation for educating. However, we are faltering in the competence produced by that capacity. Innovation is moving to other nations—for example, China and India—because they have focused on the competence of their intellectual capital. Investors will go where the intellect is, because that is the course of innovation.

Today's American students are increasingly tuned to popular culture (hip-hop)—celebrities, athletes, social media, entertainment. Education has not kept up with its mission of competence, while other mountains of culture are performing at a high level of excellence. The result is a growing incompetence in the work product of educators.

Our students need core competencies in core subjects. Without that, they are at the mercy of cultural influences which require character to withstand. Through diligence, students must develop their ability to study, to learn, to apply the resulting knowledge, and to solve the problems they face both today and tomorrow.

A CRISIS OF COMPETENCE

Competence is needed as an individual to remain necessary, to create growth and opportunity for oneself and others. Additionally, competent individuals create a competent nation. Without competence, students are left behind. And if they don't catch up, they sink. Without a competent workforce, a nation falls behind.

Education is the critical component to a successful nation, and our Christian faith must be the cornerstone for Christians.

In my experience with students, I have found that maturity is required to develop competence. Students must mature earlier. Students need to be held to a high standard from kindergarten onward and expected to perform at the highest levels. They must become self-directed and independent learners. To aid the development of maturity, discussions between students and their parents about their goals and progress toward meeting their goals should be a common occurrence.

Truthfully, weekly discussions about education are not happening in most households today, but they should be. Change is critical, imperative, if this and future generations are to lead America into the future and keep our country ahead globally. Today, more and more high school students compete globally for domestic college placement. College graduates find themselves committing with international students for domestic jobs. These days Chinese students are scoring higher on the ACT in English than our own students.

Our nation experiences tension in the unequal treatment that groups can receive. Racism in a discussion of competence manifests as the systematic denial that prevents a person from realizing the promises of our nation because of a matter outside their ability. Bad education policy handicaps opportunity, and produces incompetent students.

In one case, students were admitted who did not meet the standard and therefore were unlikely to succeed. In 2020, the Department of Justice ruled that Yale illegally discriminates against White and Asian students in its undergraduate admissions process. Further, the Department of Justice (DOJ) said race was a determining factor in "hundreds of admissions decisions" annually. The DOJ's press release on their findings reported that one-tenth to one-fourth of White or Asian students were only one-tenth to one-fourth as likely to be admitted as Blacks with similar resumés. [https://www.cnbc.com/2020/08/13/yale-illegally-discriminates-against-white-and-asian- students-justice-department-says.html.]

Parents and students, along with educational leaders, must understand the importance of competing in the marketplace and the role of education preparing them now and in the future.

Student competence that results from effective education determines in large part the return society realizes from their citizens, human capital, or human resources. And today more than two-thirds of students taking the ACT do not meet the benchmark for competence in core subject areas. This alarming statistic is worth repeating. *More than two-thirds of ACT takers do not meet the benchmark for competence in core subject areas.* The ACT standard for competence in subject areas is a score of 21.25.

THE SEVEN MOUNTAINS OF SOCIETY

Our growing levels of student incompetence are not caused by our education system alone. Our village is also culpable.

To better see a complete picture of why America is falling behind, it is helpful to view our society today as a segmented whole. In the mid-1970s, Bill Bright and Loren Cunningham, the founders of Campus Crusade for Christ and Youth with a Mission, respectively, identified seven spheres, or mountains, of influence within society. These mountains must be engaged to spread the gospel or create lasting cultural change. These seven are education, religion/church, family, media, arts and entertainment, business/commerce, and government.

Each sphere plays a specific role in our society, and competes in its own performance. The Mountain of Education is responsible to educate and to deliver products and services that reach the targeted education goals and objectives. The mountains influence each other, but each performs its own mission without regard for the others. If one underperforms, as education currently does, the others fill the void.

Each mountain of society has its own function. Several perform their functions with excellence, and are outshining the underperforming education mountain. For instance, the media and entertainment mountains pursuing their missions have a superior voice in our society. This could not occur, however, if the education mountain were performing its mission. Its students have waning competence, character, diligence, and judgment. The media and entertainment mountains can thus appeal to the lowest common denominator of competence. The growing influence of those social influences then reinforce that level of competence as the acceptable standard for young people.

For example, students spend more time watching TikTok or keeping up with social media than they do on academics. In response, t.Lab requires students to measure how and where they spend their time based on a 168-hour week. The formal regimen, process, and system developed by t.Lab implements this requirement.

These imbalanced influences are not limited to the above spheres. Decreasing parental guidance on the Family Mountain is related to decreasing church membership on the Religion Mountain and the lack of guidance by church leaders. On the Business mountain, new demands arise continually, both domestically and globally. Technology is integrated to advance automation and robotics, to fill the gap of competence and character in employees. All these interact with the breakdown in delivering student competence.

Understanding requires a view from a multifaceted lens. The new paradigm must recognize how each sphere influences and impacts our students and their education.

Finally, what influence can each of these spheres in our society wield to enable every American to reach whole competence, which translates into individual, community, country, and even global success?

EDUCATION: THE FIRST MOUNTAIN

Education, the first mountain, is very high in significance. Its roots run deep in agricultural America, an issue that must be addressed as technology continues to change and shape American life. From how we receive the news and communicate with one another to how and where we shop and find information—learn—on any subject, technology is a constant presence. The world is really at our fingertips. God gave mankind dominion over the earth (Genesis 1:26-28) and it is more evident than ever. Today more than ever, the Mountain of Education can boost student competence at primary, secondary, and postsecondary levels of education.

Yet, to a large degree, with the exception of the online learning during COVID, many students are still learning with textbooks, notebook paper, and pens. For its failure to adapt to new technology, create new systems aligned with student needs, and develop competent character, the Mountain of Education has a decreasing influence on our society. Worsening the situation: educators now exclude parents and caters to students' priorities, alienating the mountains of family and religion.

Simultaneously, the ACT and other measurement tools are revealing our students' decreasing competence in major areas of academics, with African Americans performing at the lowest of the top major racial and ethnic groups.

In addition, if education's purpose is, as Dr. King said, "to create a common set of values that allows us to live together in society," it's clear this sphere is suffering greatly. Recent protests of adversarial groups, where prejudice and incompetence produce instability, though not indicative of all Americans, highlight our continuing problems and divisions.

If the educational sphere's objective is to deliver competence to students, it is failing. Academic competence is decreasing. Leadership and character competence is decreasing. If given a basic performance review, this segment of society would receive a failing grade.

Educators are dealing with a shifting population: more diverse, less Christian, with fewer universal values and beliefs. And while diversity is a strength, it does have challenges. All of these factors are contributing to a decline in competence.

Because the excellence of education is diminished, the arts and entertainment mountain and the media mountain are growing in influence. Their impact on our society is far outsized relative to education and religion. The increased centrality in our society for digital entertainment, social media, and 24/7 news result from the excellence of those mountains. Because the other mountains are not performing with excellence, such as religion, education, and family, the influence of the entertainment and media mountains is now superior. If all mountains were performing their mission with excellence, this imbalance of influence would not occur.

Instead of focusing on students, each sector is focused on maintaining the status quo or solving its problems *independently* of the education sector. For example, instead of helping students reach competence through program funding or other means, businesses are hiring competent employees who live beyond our borders, and automating systems where possible to require less manpower and less competence.

Performance shifts in industry should include and dictate an expanding set of competencies for teachers, including digital competencies not realized by teachers and schools until forced upon them by COVID-19. The pandemic revealed the gap in our ability to use technology to educate effectively; the education industry was not prepared for the pandemic, but rather woefully unprepared for the challenge of COVID. Our students are paying the price.

Beyond the influence of the pandemic, the marketplace issue has deeper and wider implications that relate to students' career choices. Our students need teachers who understand today's marketplace and the technologies and careers it makes available now. Teachers have a critical role in inspiring our students to explore fields that will lead tomorrow's world, the discoveries on the horizon.

My conversation with one student illustrates the valuable combination of existing and new—and the cost when the two are not combined. When adaptation is subordinate to old paradigms, we do not equip our students with the competence to take advantage of opportunities and horizons.

In 2019, I attended a global leadership conference in St. Louis, Missouri, which included a panel partially composed of students. The panel members answered questions by educators, and gave students the opportunity to express their opinions in response.

One young woman commented that she had recently learned how to code and liked it, but had also wanted to be a neurosurgeon, and was now unsure which career path to choose. No one on the panel offered her their feedback, so afterward I made it a point to speak to her.

I showed her a picture on LinkedIn. A neurosurgeon was using a DaVinci robot to program neurosurgery. Then I asked her, "How do you think that robot got the necessary program? Who do you think understood the type of program needed to accomplish this neurosurgery? Doctors? There's such a vast difference between neurosurgery and coding but both can work together to create needed solutions." Systems analysts, medical professionals, and others illustrate the combined efforts needed to create the final, practical, and safe application.

The point? No one had articulated to her the career opportunities from combining old and new, in this case her two fields of interest. No one had ever told her that she could combine neurosurgery with coding.

Coding is a language anyone can learn. But more than a task, it is a discipline a person develops. A solid foundation in English, Math, Reading, and Science is needed to analyze the applied needs in the business or enterprise, and integrate the code to solve those applications. The true value of coding is understanding how to use it for real-world solutions that improve health, business, and everyday life. In the case of neurology, saving lives is the result. Coding alone is one path, but can't function with excellence in the absence of understanding the end use. Educators must impart the fundamentals needed for competency, rather than cliches that warm the heart without results.

This is why it frustrates me to see initiatives such as, "Black Girls Can Code." Of course they can, but coding alone cannot solve tomorrow's problems. Understanding a company's needs and being able to design software solutions for them is what is needed. Seeing the system need must determine the application created.

Coding becomes simple implementation once an opportunity has been identified and the solution found.

The rate of change is so blisteringly fast, existing institutions are almost rendered insignificant and inconsequential. This is why those core competencies become so important. Anyone unable to read well or do math can't function with merely a task mindset. Today, an artificial intelligence application, such as ChatGPT, can create code. Anyone unable to understand the end use of the code will be out of a job, but a coder with the core competencies will be safer because of the ability to put ChatGPT and other AI resources to full use.

These issues shed light on the education mountain's failure to address performance shifts which the other mountains are developing diligently. There are myriad reasons that imbalance is now pronounced. The seven spheres do not stand independently, but each influences the others.

We need teachers and administrators to step up to the plate, so to speak, and implement creative solutions for students to learn while educators inspire them to higher achievement. We need educational leaders to provide the leadership vision and resources which parents and educators need. Technologically competent educators can teach and motivate our students. We need to put our best team on the field.

It is time to recognize the need for improved performance by the education mountain. The influence and shifts in the other mountains require adaptation by the education industry. A new paradigm of education is needed to lead students into competence, into becoming tomorrow's leaders.

The education sphere is facing substantial challenges. Paradigm shifts are needed by educational leaders, who must develop the processes and systems to implement the new paradigm.

FAMILY: THE SECOND MOUNTAIN

It is worth stating again: the Bible says parents are expected to teach their children morning, noon, and night because parents carry the manifested blessing for their children, the blessing of personal grace. The first institution ordained by God was the family.

The beginning of knowledge (or information) carries with it wisdom and insight. Knowledge comes from respect for God, and the instructional laws of parents carry the promise of personal grace. In addition, the Scriptural meaning of the head or the neck represents revelation and reputational regard. In other words, when you say you put faith above your head, it is saying that you will actually have revelation, or you'll be able to understand things other people do not. It also says that you will have reputational regard or in other words, people will see you and your reputation will have the tendency to be good. It's just like when somebody looks at somebody in his face and just says, "You know what? They just have a right face. That child seems to be a bright child," even if they never heard the child speak.

The Bible says that's the grace that comes from actually obeying parents. And then the neck represents professional persona and achievement. When you graduate from high school, college, etc., they put a sash around your neck. The neck is actually the place where your professional persona or achievement is placed: royalty, kings, ambassadors.

The Bible becomes extremely important in the education of a child. It says, number one, a respect for God is the beginning of receiving any information or revelation that will remain with a child. It's also saying that respect for God is the beginning of wisdom. In other words, wisdom, or real insight, that will guide you in life now and into the future, is taught by mothers and fathers.

It is the responsibility of mothers and fathers to teach wisdom, respect for God, that carries a promise of grace. Teachers, then, do not carry a promise of grace for their students. What that means is: what mentors teach, unless there's a real closeness, does not have a promise of grace. It has a promise of information, it has a promise of revelation, but not have a promise of grace.

Obviously then, at the very least, parents must be intimately involved in educating their children. They have to be directional and exemplary. Parents must be diligent and expect diligence on the part of their children because parents are the source of their children's grace, or manifested blessing.

Parents are not exerting their necessary influence in our society today, and we see the outcomes. The mountains that thrive with parental influence—religion, education, and family—are waning in influence. The mountains that do not rely on parental guidance—media, arts and entertainment, and business—are the superior influences today. Particularly with students, today's mountains of media and entertainment have more impact than parents and educators as well.

Beyond the moral issues with these forms of entertainment and socialization, we most certainly have a parenting paradigm problem today. We give our children the freedom to make decisions regarding education. Many parents remain uninvolved and allow their child alone or the child's school to manage their child's education. But children are not ready to make these decisions alone.

Add to this a constant access to the arts and entertainment mountain and social media, and it is clear to that parents must be more prescriptive with their children. They must turn off the TV and meet with their children at least once each week for the specific purpose of discussing their current progress at school and develop a plan for the next week.

A study commissioned by Visit Anaheim found that families spend on average only thirty-seven minutes of quality time together on weekdays. [https://www.studyfinds.org/american-families-spend-37-minutes-quality-time/], while Edsurge reported pre-COVID that on average teens spent seven hours a day in front of a computer [https://www.edsurge.com/news/2020-09-23-childs-are-spending-more-of-their-lives-online-teachers-can-help-them-understand-why.]

Parents must accept the mantle of leadership. They must be intimately involved in the details of their children's education and provide their children the guidance they need to understand the importance of education.

RELIGION: THE THIRD MOUNTAIN

Of all seven mountains of society, before education, family and church impact our children most. Parents within the family have the greatest influence—recall the biblical mandate to teach morning, noon, and night—followed by the church, who is to teach parents and their children about Christ, what He stood for, and how to interpret the Scriptures.

But the church must guide parents and students to value education and fulfill their roles as parents and children. The church should also ensure their members know the standards Christ set for education, that His followers are to be "the head, and not the tail... above only, and not beneath" (Deut. 28:13 NKJV). Churches should teach that believers are expected to grow in Christ.

The Bible tells us that God will give us shepherds after His own heart. Yet, the church is not leading our families into increased grace and wisdom today. The purpose of the church is, in part, to inform the family with truth, to prepare families to succeed, to live in a kingdom economy. The church's lack of teaching, guidance, and influence upon families and education contributes to our students' declining competence, which causes strain on the Mountain of Education.

It is critical that the church influence our young. The church should be the main influencer of our children. church and faith should be held up, esteemed. Our leaders should be respectable and respected. We always dressed up for church. Today the church is disrespected among the younger generations. From the type of dress to music, movies, social media, church is not directing our youth into lives of integrity, pushing them to excel in character and academics and in godliness.

Godliness is living in a way that reflects the nature of Christ— treating others as you wish to be treated, caring for our neighbor, telling the truth, and so on. But the church should also diligently develop both academic competence and character traits that ensure our students grow into competent leaders.

To reach this competence, church participation must be a priority for parents. The church must accept their responsibility to our children and support parents, helping them understand and accept their mantle of leadership. Parents must rear our children to possess irreproachable character and to strive for academic excellence.

How can the church make this happen? By informing, encouraging, and supporting parents through education, groups, and opportunities. In turn, parents and families need to make church an important part of family life. Church should be the center of our communities as they lead the young to excel in both in character and academics. We must make church the center of our culture and neighborhoods, of our communities once more. A church influence on a child will help parents instill godly character and leadership skills, both critical components of whole competence. This sphere of our village should wield a weighty influence on our students. Yet, unfortunately, that is not the case today.

Instead of increasing, church attendance is decreasing, which means the mountain of religion is playing a decreasing role in shaping our students today. According to a 2019 Gallup poll, church membership decreased 20 percent in the years between 1999 and to 2019, from 70 percent to now only 50 percent of Americans who attach themselves to any type of church. [https://news.gallup.com/poll/248837/church-membership-down-sharply-past-two-decades.aspx] Most of the decline, according to Gallup, is results from the increase in people who associate with no religion. While there are reasons for this, church and faith should still be the center of our homes.

Religion is and must be a critical component of a family's life, a child's life. Church is the closest community support a parent or parents have to help instill values that form a child's character. As primary educators, parents must make faith—including church—a priority in family life.

The church must accept their role and work to reach the students in their communities. Isaiah 58:12 says the people of God are responsible to repair the breaches in society. Yet the religion mountain is largely failing to influence our families positively. This breakdown of church influence also impacts the education mountain.

ARTS AND ENTERTAINMENT: THE FOURTH MOUNTAIN

There is no doubt that arts and entertainment wield an unequal impact on our students. This sphere wields the most influence on our students. Too often our entertainment culture influences our children more than parents—consider that our children go to high-profile entertainers for relationship advice, for example, not parents or their pastor. The decline of faith-focused parenting occurs as more and more families are withdrawing from their Christian faith.

A critical lack of vision in our education industry, vision that can produce a plan and propel progress, is contributing to our decline in competence.

Steadily decreasing academic competence manifests the lack of godly character, competition, and leadership skills. Some may argue that the arts and entertainment industry contributes more than any other mountain to students' decreasing competence. This could only occur in the absence of performance by the spheres of family, church, and education.

Today, a portion of the arts and entertainment sphere promote amoral, self-focused lifestyles that remove personal responsibility from the individual to lift up society as a whole. Students consume the product of this industry, and in turn, society experiences a shift in values that impact society greatly. Because the influence is unchecked by competent parenting, education, and religious leadership, success in the arts and entertainment mountain wins influence.

The decrease in educational competence has been a concern for decades, and simultaneously there is a decrease in leadership and character competence. We are, after all, what we consume. And today's arts and entertainment industry is teaching our students to be consumers.

Increasingly, our students base their identity and future plans on what culture says to them. Fame, from YouTubers to rappers to high-level gamers, is today's hope for many students. The performance of the entertainment mountain shows a greater reward today for fame and beauty versus the hard work of acquiring the credentials needed for the top jobs centered around math and science.

Obviously, the allure of fame or success in video games is deceptive. Fame or success in these areas come to only a few, and thus the popularity of such ambitions among our young is detrimental to society as a whole. We are experiencing too much lost potential.

The issue facing us now is the imbalanced influence of each mountain. The religion and family mountains must increase their own capabilities, and compete with the other mountains. As these two mountains gain influence, the arts and entertainment mountain will respond. As a result, content can increase which helps students achieve competence, both in character and education. If this sphere shifted its focus to delivering engaging, academic content that exemplifies strong character and leadership, our students would easily be impacted.

MEDIA: THE FIFTH MOUNTAIN

Media today is another heavy influencer. Media encompasses both the news, which is increasingly polarized by perspective and opinion rather than fact, and social media that allows students to be content creators. Students today have a platform to promote themselves however they choose. From makeup artists to aspiring rappers to comedians to, well, just about everyone social media.

There is a downside: Twitter, TikTok, SnapChat, Facebook, and the other social media sites for students increasingly allow contributors to provide false, misleading information, which is creating cultural friction. At the same time, the drive for social media popularity is producing a youth culture that increasingly values superficial elements of our culture instead of lasting relationships built on honesty, integrity, and genuine care for fellow man.

Our media culture is reflecting the PISA findings noted earlier, that American students are today less likely to correctly interpret written information to determine the difference between fact and opinion than students in other countries including China, the UK,

Australia, Japan, and more. [https://www.nytimes.com/2019/12/03/us/us-students-international-test-scores.html.]

With borderless information and lack of media accountability— journalistic integrity— these issues have serious implications.

Our media sphere needs to consider how best they can use their influence to encourage content that promotes higher education, that lifts up diligent, committed students of strong character and a stellar work ethic who are poised to lead in top industries in the future. The mountain of media itself requires a population of competence if it is to remain influential.

GOVERNMENT: THE SIXTH MOUNTAIN

The Mountain of Government at every level has a job to do. Government impacts the education sphere greatly. Unlike church and family, government must be the voice of all Americans. Consequently, the federal government ensures all students have access to a quality education. State and local government, however, has a more direct role with greater impact. At this level curricula is developed, both by government and outside organizations, and decisions are made regarding how education is delivered to students.

State and local governments have the critical role of overseeing student education through public and private schools throughout the state. Curriculum, to some degree, is different from state to state or county to county. Today, thankfully, Common Core standards help affirm what students should know to be competent in core subjects. Forty-one states have currently adopted Common Core standards. Yet issues remain.

Government then has a leading role in the education of students. From student access to a quality education, to what students learn when, to where and how they learn, government is involved. Private schools are also regulated by state and local governments, and these must meet or surpass minimum requirements relating to student education and achievement.

Government then, within their constraints, should play a role in changing education to ensure American students reach competence. Government spends over 6 percent of America's gross domestic product on education. Annually, the government spends about $79 billion on education [https://www.newamerica.org/education-policy/topics/school-funding-and-resources/school-funding/federal-funding/] so this sector is a major contributor, but its influence is not producing competence overall.

Government funds are taxpayer funds, and our government is comprised of American taxpayers, thus excellence should be the expectation—and the standard.

BUSINESS: THE SEVENTH MOUNTAIN

Again, businesses have noticed the growing incompetence in America's workforce and have responded with increased certification requirements for employment. American businesses are also hiring more international employees for non-manufacturing roles, including for administrative, IT, and human resources needs. Businesses seek profit, and therefore utilize the cheapest labor and incur the least cost possible, except in high-value fields where they value expertise.

The business or commerce mountain impacts students and family because this is where jobs are. Thus, this mountain places demands with respect to skills and knowledge, demands that are accelerating as technology integration occurs. If US students lack the necessary skills and knowledge, employers go elsewhere. Businesses will look to alternative sources, international sources, to meet labor demand.

Such interdependence among countries is sometimes beneficial, but in today's world, other countries are vying to replace the leadership of America on the world business stage. Unless we increase our students' academic competence, America could be replaced as the seat of economy, innovation, and excellence.

Beyond the tutoring and test preparation segment within the business sector, every business has an interest in the collective success of every American student. The continued success of the Business mountain—indeed every segment's success—depends on student competence, not unmerited high grade point averages. High-performing students become high-performing employees who in turn create or work for businesses that realize a return. From increased profit to contributing to the well-being of society as a whole, businesses must influence the education sector, must help the education sector achieve the performance shifts necessary that will fuel business success both now and in the future.

Many corporations actively donate to educational causes. Unfortunately, their giving is not determined by results of competence. Appendix Two is an open letter by two other leaders and me, proposing four questions every corporate donor to education must ask themselves.

Non-Minorities dominate the decision-making about educational philanthropy, but have pushed back against methods that don't fit the outdated educational paradigm. Therefore methods requiring rigor, discipline, and obedience—such as those developed by t.Lab—are often regarded as too harsh. As a result, a failing educational program can receive large grants, because they fit the existing education paradigm. In contrast, a program with success after success, such as t.Lab, is repeatedly denied.

Achieving student competence will require businesses to adopt the new paradigm for competence, and be increasingly involved in education. If C-suite executives used the same paradigm for their public education engagement they use for their own children, including rigor, discipline, and high expectations, the education mountain would be far more excellent. Business philanthropy for education must include accountability for producing competence, for helping educators understand the needs of business, and for creating the drivers of student competence.

UNEQUAL BUT IMPACTFUL INFLUENCE

While each sphere has an unequal influence in student competence today, each has a role. If our goal is to create competent students, then it is past time for each mountain of society to effectively work together with the education sector—that is, if our goal is to create competent students.

Currently, parents and churches need to recapture the role as primary educators and influencers of our students. Parents and churches need to replace the heavy influence exerted by the media and arts and entertainment segments. Beyond this, government must explore and implement current drivers of education to effectively influence student competence. Government, as the primary funder and facilitator of education, must change, must produce effective systems that deliver positive results.

CHAPTER 6

COMPETENCE VERSUS DIVERSITY, EQUITY & INCLUSION

The next question that needs to be addressed is this: Is it feasible to think all students can reach competence?

YES!

I would say that not only can every student reach competence, but every student MUST also reach a basic level of competence in order to survive in both the worlds of today and tomorrow.

In an information-based society can a person survive without a basic level of competence?

NO! Here is a real-life example. Singapore initiated effort to transform their culture and economy based on market demands. Recognizing their issue with competence, its leaders made a massive effort to prepare leaders and technicians who are technology competent. Singapore is now one of the richest nations on the earth, in the top ten for billionaires per capita.

This is a life-or-death situation for our schools, families, churches, businesses... for every mountain.

COMPETENCE IS THE KEY

We are in competition with other nations, based not on diversity or equity or inclusion, but on competitive strength and intellectual capital. Capitalism is market-driven and never more so than today's connected world. Competence wins by attracting a higher monetary valuation.

Competence is excellence in performance, excellence that is impartial and independent of race, gender, sexual orientation, or financial disposition. It is the ability to realize an equitable balance between all these factors without discrimination while ensuring that no one is left behind.

Competence is the platform for true equality, diversity, and inclusion. In our ever-changing world, where excellence and competitiveness are highly valued, competence is rewarded with greater opportunity.

Competence goes beyond mere aptitude in a specific field; it means having the right skill sets and knowledge to be successful regardless of background. It means being able to perform tasks with excellence and adapting to new situations quickly. Competence allows people from all walks of life to compete on equal footing for opportunities in the workplace—whether it's getting a job, a promotion, or even starting their own business.

Competence also promotes mutual respect and understanding between individuals from different backgrounds. While race, gender, sexual orientation, and financial disposition can act as barriers to inclusion and understanding, competence allows us to see past these surface-level differences and appreciate what makes each of us unique. By focusing on excellence rather than superficial divides, we can create an environment where everyone has the same chance at success regardless of who they are or where they come from.

Ultimately, competence is the key to unlocking true equality, diversity, and inclusion in our society. With excellence in performance comes a greater appreciation for everyone's contribution, no matter their background—leading to a more unified and open society. By focusing on competence, we can create a level playing field for everyone to achieve excellence regardless of race, gender, sexual orientation, or financial disposition.

This is not only the path to true equality but also a way of creating a brighter future where all people benefit from being part of an inclusive culture that values excellence and excellence in performance above all else. It's time to move away from superficial divides and recognize excellence as the only real measure of success. Through excellence in competence, we can ensure that everyone has a fair chance at achieving their goals regardless of who they are or where they come from. That's how we will unlock true equality, diversity, and inclusion—by prioritizing excellence in performance and competence.

THE PROOF OF EXPERIENCE

t.Lab is diverse. We work with children and families representing multiple races, ethnicities, and many income levels from around the globe. Our reach and diversity give us a broad vantage point from which to view the effectiveness of our current education system.

Our t.lab faith-enabled curriculum is designed to create and propel self-directed learners to success. We first teach students how to learn and then our analysts, facilitators, mentors, and tutors facilitate the learning process. Our focus is on engaging parents and motivating students to excel and providing a resource for applying the disciplines we teach.

t.Lab's curriculum is designed for a student to achieve competency in core subjects quickly. We expect our students to achieve competency in a grade level every three months, which translates to twelve grades in four years. This assumes the newly enrolling student will be performing at the required grade level. Sadly, 75 percent of students who are behind upon leaving the third grade will never catch up.

The t.Lab model is based on research revealing that one hour of quality tutoring per week equals students completing five grades per year. t.Lab benchmarked Ivy League Tutoring on the South Side of Chicago for this metric. t.Lab adapted the standard and expectation of two hours of quality tutoring a week and students will complete three grades per year—operating as required at each grade level. The ideal t.Lab student will enter our program in second grade and t.Lab expects that the student will finish all twelve grades and be college-ready by the end of sixth grade. College readiness is measured by conducting a practice ACT test, and students are expected to realize a minimum 21.25 which is the competence benchmark for the ACT.

Every three months, as a child pursues completing a grade level, t.Lab meets with the student and parent to review the student's progress. In addition, each week the parent and child are required to meet and review the child's work to identify issues and gauge progress.

t.Lab has been called an after-school program on steroids. Country Day is a high-performing private Michigan school system. Bishop Ben Gibert, a supporter of ours, described t.Lab this way: t.Lab together with the public school produces Country Day Competence. We are not a school, and while some have suggested we form a school, we believe we are where we need to be. We work with children outside of their normal school hours, both in our technology lab in Garden City, Michigan, and digitally across the world.

FOUR PREVAILING TENDENCIES

The first, a tendency toward division, has devastated education in the African American community. Disparities among gender, race, and sexual orientation alone don't provide the insights that are necessary to establish and solve any problems that may exist. In a data-driven society, more efforts must be made to identify the root causes of any and all differences. The divisions are causing us to focus on symptoms and not problems; subsequently, the problems will remain, and the divisions will grow. These divisions are convenient excuses that prevent an intelligent response to identifying and solving problems impacting poor performance in academia by African American students.

The second tendency is towards unrighteous leadership, which has further exacerbated this issue. As leaders—both within the community and without—fail to prioritize their constituents' needs; they do not invest in the quality of educational resources for African American students. Racism exists, of course, but the unrighteousness is to blame racism for everything. Using this excuse is tantamount to hiding behind the skirts of others and surrenders the control of African American education to the very ones we blame for racism. The solution is to move forward anyway without waiting on racism to vanish.

This lack of investment leads to a cycle of poverty, as these young people are unable to gain access to higher education or gainful employment opportunities. This, in turn, creates an even larger divide between Black and white households in terms of economic standing.

The third tendency: wanting something for nothing. This has also had a detrimental effect on education in the African American community. While some individuals may have access to educational resources, they often lack the motivation and dedication to using them effectively. This issue is compounded by a pervasive attitude of entitlement that pervades many impoverished communities. It is not limited to young people; this expectation is multi-generational, creating an environment of complacency and ultimately limiting the potential for educational success for the entire African American population.

Finally, the murderous tendency has had a devastating effect on education in the African American community. Violent crime and gang activity have taken a toll on many of our communities' youth, leading to both physical and mental destruction. Those who are fortunate enough to remain safe often still face an uphill battle when it comes to accessing quality educational resources, as violence in their neighborhoods can lead to a lack of trust and investment from the government. Exacerbating the devastation of this behavior is the silence of real leadership by those in a position to reverse it.

In conclusion, division, unrighteous leadership, wanting something for nothing, and murderous tendencies have all had a tremendous impact on access to quality education in the African American community. These issues are deeply entrenched in our society and must be addressed if we are to create real and lasting change. By investing in the quality of our educational resources and providing support for young people from all backgrounds, we can ensure that no one is left behind when it comes to achieving their dreams. With this collective effort, we can work towards a brighter future for everyone.

COMPETENCE INCLUDES DIVERSITY

Our ability to remain at the forefront means seeing our educational model from a new perspective so we can recognize what is necessary to increase the ACT scores of all races and ethnic groups. Our various American demographic groups do not need an advantage over others dependent upon circumstance. Each group comes to education with its own challenges and circumstances; obstacles are overcome with character that produces competence, and diversity follows competence.

We need competence in core subjects taught in primary, secondary, and postsecondary schools, and I *know* competence is within every child's grasp.

Accepting that every student cannot realize the ACT benchmark is tantamount to failure and indicative of a system that requires major transformation. Competence in English, math, reading, and science must be a mandatory requirement for any nation seeking to compete on a global stage. In 2014 the GED (General Education Diploma) assessment test was revised to reflect current high school Common Core standards for non-traditional high school students.

Soon after, complaints arrived saying the test was more difficult than the standards required to earn a traditional high school diploma. It was more difficult to pass the GED than it was to graduate from high school traditionally. However, the more challenging GED exam had a positive effect. "We've gotten hard data back from a number of states showing that GED grads are not just performing on par, but better than high school graduates when it comes to college," C.T. Turner says, a spokesperson for the GED Testing Service.

However, because of the complaints about the test's difficulty, test developers lowered the pass score 5 points from 150 to 145, saying this was more in line the ability of a normal high school graduate. A passing score of 145, he says, puts GED holders more in line with a typical high school graduate.

Bishop Ben, the t.Lab supporter mentioned above, preached a sermon I'll never forget. He shared his testimony about not being confident that he could succeed in a high school advanced placement chemistry course and wanted out. At that time, his high school was a predominantly white school in Evanston, Illinois. Instead of telling his mother the truth, that he was afraid of failure, he told her he thought he was not wanted there, so he could get out of the class.

"Okay," his mom said.

The next day as he was walking to his chemistry class he ran into his mother and teacher conversing in the hallway. At that time Bishop Ben's mom did not even have a GED. Still there was no way she was going to let her son not take advantage of being in an advanced chemistry class. His lie revealed, his mom made him stay in the class.

Bishop Ben's testimony is a consistent testimony of the African American community rolling out of Jim Crow, rolling out of Reconstruction, when people could be murdered for trying to learn to read. So parents, determined to change their children's futures, were fierce. They were determined to ensure their children would have a better life than their own.

The same thing was true with my grandparents and with my parents. They all demanded academic excellence. Even though our parents didn't necessarily have the intimate insights and mechanics, they knew their children's success in life was predicated on getting something out of higher learning institutions. Roadblocks did not matter. They were going to try to remove any roadblocks their children faced. In the same way, their children's behavior was not going to be a roadblock for them. That is truth.

Bishop looked at me, telling his story, started to get passionate. Yelling, "DR. NIXON, MY MOM MADE ME...." The result of his parents' diligence was that in one generation, all four of his parents' children went to a tier one university, such as Princeton, Michigan, Kettering University, and Yale Law. All because their parents made them do what was best for their futures instead of what their children felt they could accomplish at the moment.

Parents today are not expecting, we are not *demanding*, that our children take education seriously in the same way our own parents did. What is the result? Incompetence, which translates into the challenges we see within society today. Just turn on the television and you'll see this truth. Every night on the news there is a murder here, a theft there—to me this is indicative of failed school systems and of incompetence.

When I went to school, home life wasn't necessarily perfect. There were higher incidences of abuse, because it was just a natural coming out of Jim Crow, yet we have to look at census data. But just understanding the conditions as a people that we were coming out of, it couldn't have been all roses, a perfect life. But still, there was this commitment on the part of parents that their children would and have a better life. Mom or Dad would just remove "you" from being your own roadblock in your life.

MOTHER PICKARD SEIZES THE MOMENT

Mother Pickard seized the moment when she saw her son, William Pickard, slipping through the cracks of his high school curriculum. She knew that he had academic brilliance and drive beneath the surface, but he needed guidance to help him discover it. She dedicated herself to obtaining the resources and support that her son needed to be accepted into a community college, although the high school guidance counselor did not believe that William Pickard could do college work. Mother Pickard convinced the guidance counselor to write a letter of recommendation while pursuing an opportunity for her son to attend Mott Community College on a "probationary status."

William Pickard made it through the "probationary period," graduated from Mott Community College, and went on to graduate from Western Michigan University, the University of Michigan, and the Ohio State University, earning the Associates, Bachelors,

Masters, and PhD degrees. Dr. William F. Pickard, as he is known today, is a successful entrepreneur, businessperson, critically acclaimed author, orator, college professor, philanthropist, and global leader. Dr. Pickard holds major interest in entertainment, manufacturing, news media, and retail markets. He has the thirteenth largest African American business in the United States.

Mother Pickard's parental excellence and unwavering diligence are an inspiration to any parent confronted with similar obstacles. Her single-minded vision for her son ultimately paid off, as William Pickard was accepted into college and eventually became Dr. William F. Pickard, a successful global leader and model of excellence, respected and loved by many. Her story serves to remind us that with vision, dedication, and guidance, parents can set their children on a path to transformation and success.

A scene in the movie *Crazy Rich Asians* depicts the Asian mother criticizing her son's successful Asian American wife for being "American"—a revealing portrayal of the difference between Asian and American parenting. The mother distinguished between Asian parents who are very involved in their children's lives, and an Asian American mother who would not have the same attitude.

I find this true with the American parents I work with. Too often their child has the freedom to make decisions they are not prepared to make wisely.

CHAPTER 7

WHAT'S WRONG WITH EDUCATION FOR AFRICAN AMERICANS?

As an African American myself, I know I experience life differently than other Americans. From my vantage point it seems that many of us have an image, a believed, shared reality of America that is inaccurate. We have been taught untruths and are slowly emerging from darkness. Dr. King is quoted, "Truth crushed to earth will soon rise again." The truth is rising.

We are seeing the racial division that still exists in America, highlighted in many public events. As the Bible says, a kingdom divided cannot stand. One example why these opposing views of America exist is seen in the actions of some Americans and groups throughout the years. For example, the Daughters of the Confederacy wrote American Civil War curriculum that purposefully downplayed the evils of slavery and wrongly shaped students' views.

This group did this because as Reconstruction came about, slaves became politicians and business owners. Former slaves began to enjoy the American way of life. When African Americans were provided real opportunities, they mastered those opportunities and did exceptionally well. The book *Southern Black Creative Writers, 1829–1953* highlights pre-Civil War African American writers who had mastered their craft—*prior to* the Civil War. Even the threat of death did not deter some African Americans from reading and writing— from mastering their craft.

Then Reconstruction was a success, which threatened the accepted way of life for many. Atrocities were many and horrific, yes. But many African Americans revealed their resilience, intelligence, ingenuity, and courage. My ancestors refused to give up or accept defeat, and their courage, strength, faith, and intelligence paved the way for their children and their children's children to be successful.

These same qualities in the African American community are needed for our students today. Placing more emphasis on competence while driving and sustaining academic systems of excellence and cultural paradigm change: that's what must be done.

CIVIL RIGHTS MOVEMENT: ADVANCING THE CAUSE

The Civil Rights Movement of the 1960s opened doors of opportunity for African Americans that had been previously unavailable. The legal framework for racial equality was established, creating an unprecedented wave of progress and advancement in civil rights.

However, it is essential to understand that this social transformation did not happen overnight; it came from a long-term commitment to pursue academic excellence, innovation, and a drive to deliver results. African Americans must continue to pursue the path of power through the same commitment, focus, competitiveness, and value that has been demonstrated throughout the civil rights era.

Academic excellence is at the core of successfully advancing in education and achieving success beyond it. Aspiring African American students should seek out educational opportunities that will help them gain the knowledge, skills, and training to thrive in their chosen fields. Furthermore, pursuing innovation is a key factor in driving progress and achieving success. Innovation allows for new solutions to be discovered that may ultimately benefit individuals, communities, and entire societies.

Every African American must understand the importance of collaboration to develop meaningful relationships with those who can act as mentors and provide the necessary guidance for professional development. These networks of strong relationships can help individuals navigate their way to the highest levels of power and transcend social constructs that limit progress and success.

We see this happening in the mountain of arts and entertainment, which includes music and athletics. The hip-hop community is driving a sustained collaboration among all entertainers, and black athletes are acting as accountability partners for each other. These collaborative efforts produce a level of wealth that few thought possible.

In conclusion, the Civil Rights Movement opened doors of equality and opportunity for African Americans. To remain competitive in a world where power is concentrated in the hands of a few, more African Americans must harness the same commitment to excellence, innovation, and networking that has been demonstrated throughout history. Only then can true equality be achieved.

On the African American Experience of America: A Third Reconstruction

The Civil Rights Movement, which I term a "second reconstruction," was from 1955 to 1968. This was a movement that ended legal segregation and fueled new laws upholding civil rights. The movement, with Dr. Martin Luther King Jr. as one of its leaders, further elevated the need for equal rights and inspired a people to believe in a country that could ultimately live up to its creed.

Upon us now, I believe, is the Third Reconstruction, and this reconstruction is one that has the promise of bringing more equality. Know this. Believe this. Equality, achieved equity, and fairness will make student competence even more critical. As equals, everyone competes by the same standards.

In this Third Reconstruction, excellence in education—as measured by African American competence—must be a critical priority. Real equality will be found in academic excellence and intellectual capital. More Americans need to recognize this. In this new America, people will be largely separated between the intelligent and the ignorant, the competent and the incompetent.

As the conversation about our Third Reconstruction progresses, our focus must include assimilating African Americans to power in our society, and addressing the gaps in diversity, equity, and inclusion. A top priority and pathway to achieve that is growing our academic capacity and increasing our intellectual capital.

Without access to power, we cannot rightfully compete, contribute, and improve the greatest country that has ever existed: America. Our nation is the most competitive in history, yet offers access and opportunities for those who can't compete.

When equality exists, we all learn and accept the same standards. America offers opportunity fairly well. In the wake of WWII, Jews wanted to come here for opportunity. Asians, and all nationalities are coming to America today for opportunity still. However, they are all prepared to compete for it.

The *Federalist Papers* says that the American system depends on our people remaining honest, and I cannot say we have been honest about our racial issues. Yet we must be honest if we are to work together for a prosperous America now and in the future. I believe the system has intentionally omitted African Americans from the opportunities extended to other races and nationalities. One evidence is the failure to compensate African Americans for labor alone which would measure in the trillions of dollars, not to mention the many atrocities.

However, African Americans have made tremendous gains in spite of the inequalities and have forced our nation to live by its own creed and laws, both through the Civil Rights Movement and through ongoing efforts. The trend is not merely equality for African Americans, but for all Americans, when the principles of our founding credo are integrated in our society. We need to be honest with ourselves and one another about this issue, and work toward competence and academic excellence for all.

Statistics show that the greatest growth in the African American middle class has occurred in the country since the assassination of Dr. King. It is almost like there was guilt that fueled this growth, as access to resources and opportunities were more greatly extended to African Americans. But guilt and sympathy are not the same as equality. And truthfully, what I hear still today in the voices addressing unequal opportunities for the American way, and the systematic denial of resources, is guilt. What's lacking is an understanding of the real causes of inequality in America. That's why the problems persist and worsen. The solutions offered from a guilt motivation aren't addressing the real barriers.

UNDERLYING CAUSES: ORIGIN CONTEXTS

The contexts from which African Americans, Europeans, Asians, Indians, and Jews have migrated to America have a lasting effect on their ability to assimilate into American society and access to power. The different contexts from which minority groups have migrated to America should not limit their ability to succeed in this country; rather, it should be used as a means of recognizing the unique experiences of each group and working to provide them with the resources they need to prosper.

African Americans were brought to America as slaves with no intention of improving their own lives; they were used to make life better for others. In contrast, the other groups came to America in search of opportunity, the chance to improve their lives and those of their families.

The historical context of African Americans has impacted their academic competence and competitiveness compared to other groups. The origin of their coming to this nation has been internalized and handed down the generations for five hundred years. This can impair young people's internal drive for excellence.

With systemic racism embedded in American society, African Americans have had fewer resources and access than other minority groups. This includes a lack of education or limited access to higher education institutions, thereby limiting their opportunities for success.

In contrast, other minority groups have come to America with more resources and access to educational institutions that allow them to develop their academic skills and gain competitive advantages over African Americans in the job market. In consequence of their context, these non-African American groups have gained greater access to resources, educational opportunities, and job markets. All these provide advantages and a pathway to success. African Americans with their vastly difference context are easily left behind.

To ensure equity and inclusion for all people regardless of race or ethnicity, we must recognize the unique histories and experiences of each group, and work to provide equitable access to resources for those who have been historically marginalized. Only then can we truly move towards a more inclusive society that works for everyone.

With that, we can strive towards greater equality and inclusion for all. We can equally facilitate the drive for competence in all our students.

THE RICH HISTORY OF AFRICAN AMERICAN EDUCATION

Drawing on the work of Dr. James D. Anderson in "The Education of Blacks in the South: 1860–F1935," it is clear that African Americans have long had to struggle to achieve excellence in education. From the earliest efforts made by freed slaves to ensure access to books, up through the 1930s when educational opportunities were finally being provided to African Americans throughout the South, it is evident that those who were successful in their educational pursuits had a fierce determination to excel and make use of whatever opportunities were available.

Literacy rates for African Americans increased dramatically during this period due largely to dedicated teachers, administrators, and parents who fought diligently and persistently for the rights of Black students. Many of the same ideals that Dr. Martin Luther King Jr. held and preached throughout his career were echoed in the determination of these educators to ensure African American students had access to quality education.

It is important for us to remember and honor those who paved the way, through their fierce determination and dedication, for future generations of African Americans to achieve excellence in education. We owe it to them, and to ourselves, to continue the legacy that was put forth by Dr. Anderson and others who worked tirelessly to determine the successful outcome of African American educational pursuits in the South and throughout America. Let us never forget their efforts as we continue to strive for educational excellence every day.

The sacrifices of those who have gone before us should not be forgotten. Let us honor their memory and continue to build on the excellent foundation they have laid for us. We must always strive to achieve excellence in education and stay true to our commitment that no one is left behind. This is a goal we can all work towards to-gether—with courage, determination, and a burning desire to suc-ceed. We owe it to those who have gone before us, and we owe it to ourselves. Let us work together towards achieving excellence in education for all.

EDUCATION UNLOCKS COMMUNITY SUCCESS

The hidden cost of education is something that many people do not think about. When we talk about the importance of education, it's often to better ourselves and our community.

However, there are other ways in which an uneducated African American can be disadvantaged: they may have trouble finding a job due to a lack of skills or experience. They may struggle finan-cially because they cannot find employment opportunities within their desired field or at their desired pay rate. They will make less money than someone with a bachelor's degree, even if both indi-viduals work full time.

The benefits of education go beyond the individual and their community: it reduces crime rates as well as substance abuse rates. One study found that people with higher levels of education are less likely to become incarcerated, and those who do will stay in prison longer than someone without an education level above a high school diploma.

Education is the key for many African Americans: it unlocks future success and opportunities, no matter what a person's back-ground or present financial situation may be like.

BAD LANGUAGE: THE IMPACT OF THE N-WORD

The N-word has had a profound and lasting impact on society, economically, culturally, educationally, socially, and in terms of community health. Research indicates that the use of this racial slur has caused significant economic damages to individuals affected by it as well as to entire communities. This is due to both direct costs and indirect losses from discrimination.

Those costs include suppressed education. Research reveals that the N-word has been linked to lower reading levels among African American students and higher dropout rates in some school districts. A hostile learning environment for students results when this word is used, whether formally or informally, in every aspect of life, especially among African Americans. This leads to poorer academic performance for all students. Additionally, studies suggest that the use of the N-word may lead to decreased competition and reduced economic opportunities for individuals in affected communities.

If JFK's principle is true, that a rising tide floats all boats, the opposite must hold true as well. School leadership that tolerates such a blanket slur for some of its students will find all its students weighed down.

The extensive economic costs alone illustrate the poverty inflicted when racial slurs manifest divisive racism. Studies show increased discrimination and decreased economic competitiveness where the N-word is in use. African American students experience higher dropout rates in such school districts, leaving them less prepared with the competence to contribute.

The expense of tolerating this racial slur is also borne by our entire culture. The N-word has been linked to increased feelings of insecurity, alienation, and anger among those who are targeted by it. This racial slur is used as a tool of oppression and humiliation. Furthermore, research indicates that the use of this word can lead to increased stress levels and negative mental health outcomes among those affected.

Our young people are forming their identity, ambitions, and dreams. Clearly, the oppression of such a slur hurts our entire society by impairing their ambition to contribute, saddling them with anger, and pushing them into dead-ends of despair.

Community health is also adversely impacted by the use of the N-word. Because it reinforces stereotypes and marginalizes certain groups, this pejorative insult spreads divisiveness like a cancer throughout neighborhoods. Evidence also suggests that crime and violence increase in communities where the word is tolerated.

The Bible describes people "whose consciences have been seared as with a hot iron" (1 Tim. 4:2). When this n-word is used among African Americans, it sears their own consciences. As a result, they can use the offensive word without any conscience, unaware that it's wrong and damaging. The searing means they lose the ability to know that the n-word is wrong. And when a conscience is seared, the impact affects everything—all from one little word used without thoughtfulness.

Given the high cost and damaging impact of this word, we must take steps to address and eliminate its use in society. Raising awareness about the harms associated with this racial slur is step one. Encouraging people to challenge language or attitudes which are oppressive or discriminatory is vital.

Our effort must not be limited to the individual level or personal interaction. Education systems must ensure that all students have a safe and inclusive learning environment. For maximum learning, safety must include freedom from racism and hatred. Lastly, we must jointly create policies to protect individuals from discrimination and to enforce intolerance for the N-word and its ways of thinking. Continual resolve in these actions will promote equity in educational and economic opportunities, with a freedom from the oppression of slurs.

The N-word's oppression has had a profound impact on our entire society. Any way you consider it, we have all suffered. African American students may be the intended victims, but the blowback effects everyone. By recognizing the damaging ripples effect of this word upon individuals, communities, and our nation, we can create a more equitable and just society. Through education, awareness, and policy change, we can work together to create a society where everyone has the opportunity to succeed and thrive.

HOW CULTURAL DEVELOPMENT IMPACTS EDUCATION IN THE AFRICAN AMERICAN COMMUNITY

Africa has been the cradle of humanity for millennia, but what does this mean to African Americans? How do we think about ourselves in relation to Africa and its history? The African American community is a product of both Africa and America. In its struggle against racism, the African American community has developed an Afrocentric culture that is distinct from other communities. Despite being one of the most well-studied groups in America, there are still many gaps in our knowledge about how cultural development impacts education for African Americans.

Educational excellence can impart cultural norms. Implicitly and explicitly, schools are one place that African American children learn expectations. All levels of schooling from pre- kindergarten through college have power to raise the bar for our students. The question is, what expectations are being perpetuated?

If the four tendencies in chapter six are not corrected, the self-reinforcing low expectations are adopted by African American students. These cultural norms shape the way students engage in schoolwork, relate with peers, learn from teachers, and express themselves academically. The foundation for these behaviors lies in creativity and expression.

The fact that schools are able to impart these powerful expectations is in and of itself an asset. We can use this knowledge as a tool for reform at all levels of schooling from pre-kindergarten through college. Technology and data can enable this reform as each student's needs can be identified and addressed.

African American culture in education has the potential to solve many of our problems in education for both African Americans and non-African Americans.

One of the more recent questions we are grappling with is how to define culture. Culture can be defined on a continuum from poverty and oppression, where there is little space for creativity or expression, to privilege and opportunity, where the opposite would hold true. There are also differences in cultural development depending on when one immigrated into America's educational system. There are differences between one's home country view of education and the cultural expectations students encounter as they become more acculturated to American schools.

The foundation for these behaviors lies in creativity and expression, which can be seen most clearly through an understanding of African Cultural Development Theory (ACDT) developed by Dr. Claude Anderson in 1994. When Blacks embrace their culture as Black persons, they are able to see themselves and the world around them through new lenses that allow for creativity and expression of who we are and what it means to be human.

This means that there is an expectation of what it means to be African American and how one should behave as such. These cultural norms shape the way students engage in schoolwork, relate with peers, learn from teachers, and express themselves academically.

At the crux stands a fundamental truth: too many African Americans have been, and continue to be, relegated to a state of permanent underclass by systemic factors that have resulted in economic disparities and opportunities. The result is an environment where some African Americans are often burdened with poverty and disengaged from the modern economy. This is not a new phenomenon, but rather one which has persisted for generations.

Despite this dire reality, I believe all African Americans have the potential to rise above these systemic barriers and achieve true excellence. To do so, we must focus on building a culture of competitiveness to outpace their peers in education and entrepreneurship. This requires proactive investments in education and resources that empower African Americans to create opportunities of their own.

ONE WHO ROSE ABOVE: THE JEWISH AMERICAN COMMUNITY

The Jewish population in the United States wields a considerable amount of power and influence. According to a 2013 Pew Forum study, 5.8 million people in the US identify as Jews by religion—representing approximately 2% of the total US population. Yet despite this small population, they exert impressive political, economic, and social clout.

The sheer contrast between their population and their outsized influence speaks volumes about what a resolute community can achieve. The Jewish community has an intrinsic commitment to faith, education, and excellence. The resulting prowess and competence among this small contingent earns them the exercise of authority in our society.

Their resolute competence produces life-sustaining power and wherewithal. They have leveraged that, together with their human capital, to become an integral part of the American political process. Their influence in support of justice reflects their powerful values.

Additionally, the Jewish American community is well-represented in businesses and corporations, often in the C-suite. Where they contribute to markets and industries, success often becomes evident. An outsized proportion of Jews are employed in managerial positions, own their own businesses, or sit on corporate boards.

American Jews also have a strong international influence, particularly in Israel. The Israeli government is heavily influenced by American-Jewish community, not only its own residents. They exercise great influence over Israel's politics and economy.

Their deep effect on America has also resulted from the Jews' commitment to philanthropy and social action. Many of our nation's major charities are funded by Jewish donors; the Jewish community actively advocates for social change through various organizations.

Overall, the 5.8 million Jews living in the US are a formidable force on both local and global scales. By a multi-generational commitment to competence, they have developed an influence out of proportion to their small numbers. Their ability to mobilize resources and influence key decision-makers is the outcome when a community has the competencies needed. This has created an impressive level of power they've used to advance their interests and beliefs. Through their faith, education, and excellence, they have established a position of dominance, and they are shaping the political and economic, both within the United States and abroad.

Other communities can take note. When its leaders exemplify a community attitude of excellence, the people advance, their wealth expands, their influence deepens. The power of the competent community is limitless.

WE CAN RISE ABOVE AS WELL

The key, then, is for African Americans to view themselves as competitive forces in the national and global economy; only by doing so can we break the cycle of poverty and unlock a path towards economic progress and prosperity. This is not an easy task, but it is one that must be undertaken if African Americans are to rise out of the permanent underclass. With dedication and a commitment to excellence, I am confident that African Americans can break this cycle and take their place as equal players in the national and global economy.

It's time for us to believe in ourselves, invest in our own success, and become competitive forces in the economic sphere. We must no longer be content to remain in a state of permanent underclass, but instead strive to attain true excellence and stand alongside our peers as equals. Through this process, we can secure our economic future and build an environment where African Americans can thrive. That is my hope for the future, and it begins with all of us taking control of our own destiny.

FATHERS AND THE AFRICAN AMERICAN STUDENT

White male college students have a clear advantage for success in STEM fields and job opportunities. Studies suggest that this is largely due to the increased parental involvement of their fathers. Fathers are more likely than mothers to exert informal influence, especially regarding major and curriculum. This commitment and drive to ensure that their sons are successful provide a better return on investment on their education, enabling them to excel in more competitive markets like STEM fields.

Furthermore, fathers also tend to be more involved financially when it comes to college expenses and can provide additional resources or connections through their networks that may not be available to students from other backgrounds. This can make all the difference for a student's success, since having access to resources and connections can give them an edge in landing internships or jobs after college.

In today's global economy, where STEM fields are becoming increasingly competitive, fathers provide an invaluable support system that gives white male college students an edge. By understanding the importance of parental involvement, especially that of fathers, we can better equip all college students with the necessary tools to compete for success in higher education and career opportunities.

By recognizing the benefit of fatherly involvement with college students, we can seize the resulting advantage. More African American fathers should encourage their children to be competent for college, and to match opportunities with intensity and character. This is exactly what occurred in past years and gave rise to the success that the African American community enjoys today.

Additional fatherly engagement with African American college students will help bridge the gap between groups with different backgrounds and resources. Because these fathers can make such a difference, our education community can strategically make it inviting for them to contribute. A more level playing field for college success can enable all students, regardless of background, to have the same chances of achieving their academic and professional goals.

Conclusion: White male college students tend to be more successful in STEM disciplines and job opportunities due to increased parental involvement from their fathers. Fathers are more likely than mothers to provide firm guidance on academics, as well as financial and social resources. By recognizing this gap and working to open the door for fathers' engagement with their students, we can create a more level playing field in higher education and job possibilities.

AN OBSTACLE TO ASSIMILATING TO POWER IN HIGHER EDUCATION: PRECONCEIVED NOTIONS

The preconceived notions about African Americans not being competent and diligent have had a disproportionate impact on the lack of opportunity for African Americans in higher education in the US. These stereotypes, perpetuated by media outlets and general American culture, have resulted in an environment where it has become increasingly difficult for African Americans to obtain access to resources that would enable them to gain the qualifications needed to qualify for higher education. This has resulted in a lack of competitiveness among African American students who, due to their perceived incompetence, are less likely to be accepted into prestigious universities and high-quality programs.

Furthermore, this perception of incompetence has extended beyond just higher education. It has resulted in an overall sense of doubt about the ability of African Americans to perform in any field, regardless of their qualifications or achievements. This has caused many educational and professional institutions to be hesitant when considering African American applicants, as they have often been deemed not to have the necessary skills and abilities as compared with other candidates.

The damaging impact of these preconceived notions is not just limited to the opportunities for African Americans in higher education. It also has a direct impact on the attitudes of society at large toward African Americans, creating an environment of distrust and lack of respect where African Americans' achievements are overlooked or disregarded. This sentiment has been perpetuated by media outlets, entertainment, and particular cultures within American society.

The stereotype of African Americans as incompetent and lacking in diligence has had a detrimental effect on their ability to assimilate into power structures within higher education in the US. It has resulted in an environment where it is difficult for African Americans to obtain the qualifications or resources needed to gain access to prestigious universities and top-level programs. This has hindered their ability to compete on a level playing field with other candidates. As such, African Americans have been disadvantaged in terms of gaining access to higher education.

In order for African Americans to gain the opportunity to attain influence within higher education, these preconceived notions about them must be addressed and challenged in order for progress to be made. Only then can African Americans truly gain access to the resources and opportunities necessary for them to excel in higher education.

THE HIDDEN TRUTH: WHY ISN'T THE BEST AFRICAN AMERICAN TALENT IN EDUCATION?

African Americans make up 13% of the total population but only 2.4% of university professors and 4.2% of college presidents. This begs the question: what is happening with all the best African American talent that could be contributing to our education system?

Where is our system for allocating talent? What drives the system: knowledge, or market, or data? The products and services offered by African American talent aren't being allocated to education. There are many highly qualified African American influencers and leaders who have great background and skills to educate others. Why aren't they in places of educational leadership?

Competing nations are a significant influence, as described elsewhere. Existing paradigms in the education system reinforce themselves.

Educational institutions may have a bias against hiring African Americans. They are often relegated to being instructors in the lower-level courses while Caucasian professors teach upper-level classes which typically pay more and come with greater prestige. African American instructors are also less likely to receive tenure than their white counterparts, even when they have a better teaching record, higher student evaluations, and better results in publishing and research.

What can be done to get the best African American talent into education? One solution is getting more minority people into higher education positions, like college deans and presidents, so they can mentor students from their own communities. Programs that place African Americans in predominantly white institutions ("PWI") should also receive funding because these institutions are often difficult places for Black students to thrive.

How we come into education can be in the right order, or the wrong order. Newly minted degreed and college graduates obtain work as teachers, for which they are not truly prepared with experience. There are many others who are far more qualified with wisdom and experience, such as military or business retirees. Corporations can lend executives to schools so that their wisdom can be passed down to students. This can occur mid-career as well as after retirement. IBM is an example on one corporation with this vision.

Such factors in combination create a downward pressure on the competency of African Americans which is self-reinforcing.

THE DECEPTIVE PERCEPTION

Parents who live in low-income neighborhoods and are struggling to meet their children's needs may think that moving to a "better" school district or spending more money on education will address the academic disparities. This perception is deceptive. The reality is that most children of color are not achieving at the same level as other students despite these efforts, and a complex set of factors are responsible for this situation.

For example, many African American children are simply not reading at the same level as their other peers before they enter kindergarten, and we know that "word gap" widens during school years. In elementary schools, some students face social barriers to learning such as feeling like an outsider or experiencing bullying, while others struggle with mathematics because they are not learning basic counting and arithmetic skills before they start school.

The problem is not how much parents spend on education but preparing and identifying the specific learning needs of their children. Parents who default to their children's uninformed, unqualified choices and decisions are leaving their children unprepared.

It is true that some schools perform better than others and parents should have the right to choose a school that meets their children's needs, but if they want to address the challenges in African American education, they need to invest in parenting education and other interventions that are not dependent on location.

A RESPONSE TO STANDARDIZED TESTING DETRACTORS

There are ACT (and SAT) detractors. I know well their arguments. Many say that the ACT and SAT are inherently racist. I disagree. I had the opportunity to be a caller on a syndicated radio talk show to discuss these tests' racial bias. When I said standardized tests aren't racially discriminatory, he responded by saying that I represent the right, and that I did not like public schools. Another comment was that I represent corporate interests. Nothing could be further from the truth.

Unfortunately, this host and others who believe the tests are biased are not helping African Americans reach competence, which is the ultimate goal. If this view, that the test is racially biased, becomes the norm, African Americans will not be aided. We *need* a benchmark to measure a student's knowledge and their ability to apply the knowledge gained. Should these tests be eliminated, more African American students might be accepted into top-tier colleges, but will they perform well there? In my experience, no—not for the most part.

It is also important to mention that the ACT is only one benchmark necessary to measure competence, and its measurement is only one point in time. It does not limit the student's potential to improve; it doesn't lock the student into the score forever. Other measurements are just as critical. Measuring other competencies are benchmarks related to competence including leadership traits, leadership competencies, and competence in technology and personal finance, and for good reason. Yes, I've heard the test doesn't always measure a student's ability. While that is true, it does measure competence in core subject areas at a point in time. It's only accurate in predicting performance during the freshman and sophomore years of college. Additionally, the student is not locked into the score and need not stay at that score.

At t.Lab, we developed gap analysis tools to identify for students where their areas of highest potential improvement can be addressed. To do this, of course, requires a paradigm for improvement which values such tools.

In response to the ACT detractors, several points need to be made. The first point relates to the reason the ACT measures competence and highlights the gap in our students' education. Curriculum such as Common Core includes both learning objectives and performance objectives. Learning objectives are things students must *understand* following instruction, and performance objectives are things students should be *able to do* following instruction. Learning objectives involve knowledge gained through facts or processes, and performance objectives are, of course, applying the new knowledge gained.

In classrooms, time allocation is focused on learning objectives at the expense of other ones. Often, performance objectives are not addressed or met, which means a test like the ACT that tests both learning (knowledge) and performance (application) ability in core subjects are difficult for students to master and realize a competent score. Students' scores indicate the numbers of students who both have the necessary knowledge and the ability to apply the knowledge correctly is shrinking.

Subjects learned but not applied are quickly forgotten. The classroom educators who excel at learning objectives can fall short on the performance objectives. This may be a factor in the grade inflation; students can remember long enough for a test but forgetting afterward, they do not develop the competency the subject was intended to produce.

The ACT assesses a student's competency level gained in English, Math, Reading, Science, and Writing, as well as a STEM metric. The score earned by the student is an indicator of expected college performance in the freshman and sophomore years, and is ultimately a reflection of the capability of our entire education processes and systems.

Currently, our consistently decreasing median scores indicate a problem within our education sector. One that needs to be solved. Our decreasing scores can be—and should be— viewed as an opportunity to be leveraged.

Tutoring and test preparation is a $1.1 billion dollar cottage industry in the United States. Twenty-five percent of that total— about $275 million dollars—is spent on test preparation. [https://www.marketwatch.com/story/some-wealthy-parents-are-dropping-up-to-10000-on-sat-test-prep-for-their-childs-2019-06-21]

Overall, the government sector spends on average 6.2 percent of the gross domestic product in the US on education, and it is estimated that each dollar spent generates a return of twenty dollars. [https://www.investopedia.com/ask/answers/020915/what-country-spends-most-education.asp]

That being the case, who should be motivated to solve the ineffectiveness in the education sector? The church and business sectors should be integral components in improving our education sector. The church has a God-given responsibility to repair the breaches in our society. Our leaders, however, often ignore these realities. Those who benefit from the ineffectiveness are those who are profiting from maintaining the status quo. Those who profit from our education system's ineffectiveness: tutoring services and test preparation services and high-performing private schools.

Underperforming students then are the ones who lose. Tutoring combined with character development yields results. If parents cannot afford tutoring or test preparation services, the character of their child can help offset this obstacle. America offers the most educational resources of any nation; services that are not affordable can often be found, nonetheless. Students succeed when they have the character to learn. Such students who need tutoring can benefit, but such assistance does not guarantee the desired result if the character is absent. It has been proven that tutoring alone is not a solution for incompetence.

Who should be motivated to solve the ineffectiveness of our systems? Whose head is stuck in the sand? Who benefits from the ineffectiveness? Who loses from the ineffectiveness?

Some believe the ACT tests a student's ability to take a test. However, life is a test every single day. Students certainly take tests at school. Beyond this, the standard deviation of the ACT is plus or minus two-and-a-half points. So a really good test taker might score two-and-a-half more points than a poor test taker when both have the same level of competence. Standard deviation measures performance against the mean.

Many believe the test to be biased. It *is* biased. The test is biased in that to score well a student must have a certain degree of knowledge. The ACT measures competence—period. It is biased if you do not have the knowledge necessary to do well. The ACT is biased in the same way football, basketball, or baseball skill is biased to the level of competition that exists.

Anything competitive is biased. It is biased if the student has not achieved competence in the subject areas tested.

Returning to the parent's God-given responsibility, Proverbs 10:4 tells us that slothfulness leads to poverty while diligence leads to wealth. The reality is that regardless of the numbers derived from tests and statistics ranking us against other countries, if parents follow the Lord's directive to teach their children morning, noon, and night, if parents remain committed to our Christian faith and teach that faith to our children, the land of the free can be a reality for all within the US, which will continue to lead the world.

Yes, parents have a pivotal role. However, "It takes a village to raise a child." It has also been argued the test is racially biased. It has been said the ACT doesn't contain racially diverse content. I don't agree with either of these arguments.

It has been argued that if a student does not have test-taking skills he or she will not perform well on the exam. These people believe the exam does not measure competence. Instead, it measures, in a large part, a student's ability to take a test. However, they have been taking these tests for years. Life is going to be a test every single day. Many issues we have are related to how we teach, what we expect from teaching, and the effort we put into it.

At the core of this issue is competition. The ACT measures competence, and students from across the world take the same test. And while America still has the greatest education capacity, but more and more international students are gaining an advantage over American students; international students are demonstrating competence, as we read earlier according to PISA, our students' decreasing competence is having a global impact.

The cost of incompetence must be recognized, faced, and addressed now to ensure our students grow into global leaders who can protect America's future and further peace in our nation and throughout the world. Without addressing this crisis, the American education system remains a threat to our national security.

[https://www.marketwatch.com/story/some-wealthy-parents-are-dropping-up-to-10000-on-sat-test-prep-for-their-childs-2019-06-21]

[https://www.investopedia.com/ask/answers/020915/what-country-spends-most-education.asp.]

THE COST OF WILLFUL BLINDNESS

The denial and/or ignorance of valid data on the performance of African American students at standardized tests has had a cancerous effect on the African American education community. This refusal to acknowledge hard facts has caused many members of this community to miss out on the opportunity to understand their own strengths and weaknesses, as well as those of their peers. Such an attitude has also had an immense impact on the mental health of African American students, as they are unable to accurately measure their academic competitiveness with other students. This refusal to face facts often leads to low self-esteem, depression, and anxiety among African American students.

The lack of accurate data in the African American education community results in a misunderstanding about what kind of education and learning would be most beneficial to students. Without reliable data, African American leaders are unable to accurately assess the needs of their communities and make appropriate decisions when it comes to educational policies. This lack of knowledge also impedes the ability for these leaders to effectively guide and motivate students in achieving their academic goals. As a result, African American students are not given the support and guidance necessary to succeed in their academic endeavors.

The consequences of denying and ignoring valid data on African American student performance is far-reaching. This lack of knowledge has caused a ripple effect that has stifled the growth of the African American education community, as well as hindered the overall success of African American students. Leaders must take it upon themselves to embrace the facts and use them to provide students with accurate guidance so that they can achieve their academic goals. Without this, African American students will continue to suffer from a lack of access to resources and support needed for success in school.

This analysis highlights the urgent need for African American leaders to embrace the facts and use them to their advantage. By doing so, leaders can provide African American students with an accurate understanding of their own strengths and weaknesses, as well as those of their peers. With this knowledge, African American students can be better equipped to make informed decisions about their education and learning, allowing them to reach their academic goals. Ultimately, this will lead to a more successful African American education community and create greater opportunities for the future of these students.

By recognizing the importance of data in the African American education community, leaders can take necessary steps towards helping their students reach success. This includes providing access to resources and support needed for academic achievement, as well as encouraging an environment that promotes growth and learning. With these efforts, African American students can be guided to success and the African American community can continue to thrive.

A thorough understanding of data is critical in providing a successful educational environment for African American students. Leaders within the African American education community must take it upon themselves to accept the facts and use them to the advantage of their students. This will help foster an environment that encourages growth and success, ultimately allowing African American students reach their full potential. For the future of the African American education community and its students, it is essential that leaders take a proactive stance and embrace data in order to help all students succeed.

TRANSFORMING OUR OWN CHILDREN
Every generation of African Americans has borne a collective responsibility to make sure that our children exploit access to high-quality education while generating greater success in academic performances. If we are going to move forward as a community, it is essential that we assemble and deploy the brightest and best professionals—teachers, administrators, counselors, coaches, and support staff—to transform education within our community in order to ensure that our children are equipped with the skills, knowledge, and confidence to compete in a globalized economy.

We must reject mediocrity and political incompetence in how education is conducted and administered within the African American community. We cannot simply accept substandard schools and limited educational resources as inevitable; we must challenge ourselves and strive for excellence. We must be bold in our commitment to the transformation of education for African American students, both within our communities and around the world.

In this effort, we must equip our children with the skills needed to succeed in a rapidly changing global economy—the ability to think critically, communicate effectively, and solve problems collaboratively. We must provide them with the tools to become responsible and contributing citizens, instilling in them a sense of purpose and a commitment to helping others. We must ensure that no child is left behind, regardless of race or economic status or culture.

It is our responsibility to create an educational system within the African American community that will enable our children—and generations to come—to compete on an equal footing with their peers around the world. We must strive to make sure that each and every African American child has to take advantage of educational resources, while leadership is driven to improve the quality and performance of education systems.

Students get the results by applying themselves and taking advantage of the opportunities. But it is up to the leaders to provide the resources and improve the quality of the systems. Leaders must be driven to improve those educational opportunities. Together, we can create an educational system that will produce exceptional students and academic results, putting them on a path to global competitiveness.

When we come together in this way, we can be sure that the transformation of education within our community will lead us to a brighter future. It is essential that every African American join together in this effort and do their part to ensure the success of our children's educational future.

Together—with our best team on the field—we can achieve excellence. But who makes up our best team?

CHAPTER 8

WHY WE MUST PUT OUR BEST TEAM ON THE FIELD

Praise the Lord.
Blessed are those who fear the Lord,
who find great delight in his commands.
Their children will be mighty in the land;
the generation of the upright will be blessed.
Wealth and riches are in their houses,
and their righteousness endures forever.
Psalm 112

"Every day you either get better or you get worse.
You never stay the same."
– Coach Bo Schembechler

I played baseball in high school and college, and along with every other athlete, fan, or coach of any sport, I will tell you that no coach *ever* put their worst players on the field. Of course they didn't. Every coach, every sports team, plays to win. They put their best team on the field. Just the same, to ensure every student wins—achieves competence in core subjects—we must put our best team on the field.

The ACT scores released October 2020 for the 2020 graduating class indicate yet another drop for ACT scores overall. An
article published by InsideHigherEd.com was titled "ACT and SAT
Scores Drop." It began, "Average ACT composite scores declined
this year from 20.7 to 20.6—the lowest level in 10 years." As recently as 2017, the score on the composite averaged 21. Note
even a 21 is not the competence mark of 21.5, and 20.6 is a long
way from our goal of a median score of 25 by 2025—not to mention
the 35 required to get into the top-Tier 1 schools.

How do we win? How do we get to a median ACT score of 25
by 2025? We begin by recognizing our weaknesses. We begin by
changing our old paradigms and forming new paradigms that help
our students rise. We begin by understanding what education is,
and by accepting the reality that our students are becoming increasingly academically incompetent.

We begin by changing or further implementing the education
drivers that produce student competence. We define what education is and develop effective delivery methods that consistently
achieve measurable results.

TEAM MEMBERS

Today, just as our education systems are not producing consistent
results, parents and their villages are suffering from failed leadership too. Failed leadership does not accept the mantle of leadership. Instead it says, "No, this is not where we're going." Parents
are not accepting the mantle of leadership. They are not engaging
with their children on an ongoing basis about their education, and
this is a costly mistake.

Parents *must* accept the mantle of leadership. Parents must
lead their children to competence through diligent parenting—being involved and helping their children develop their strengths
and overcome their weaknesses. Weekly meetings regarding only

education should be the norm in the home. Parents should help their students make informed decisions regarding college early, which will help them reach their goals.

Parents cannot do this alone. The African proverb we've all heard, "It takes a village to raise a child," is true. We already touched on this idea in the Introduction and in Chapters Three and Five. Parents are only one of the seven spheres in society needed to enable a person to reach whole competence.

A SUCCESSFUL PARENTING PARADIGM

God also says the parent has the responsibility for educating their children. Just as creation began with a couple who then became a family, all change is rooted in the family. Culture, education, government, and even church is rooted in the family. Family came first, so families dictate culture, which creates all things, society, education, and the rest. God made a covenant with a couple in the garden, then he made a covenant with a family, Noah and his family, then a tribe, Abraham, then a nation, Moses, and then a kingdom, David, then a church, Jesus. Life begins in the family. Thus, parents are the primary educators of their children. While this may not be the primary view for everyone today, it is biblical.

Parents should know what their children are learning, what books they are reading, what they are watching on TV, where the child should go to college for the best results. Parents should guide the family and children so that college is a priority, and the only option for advancing the family.

The next question is, "How do I as a parent ensure my child or children develop the educational competence they need in elementary and high school to ensure success in college?"

The parents' answers to these questions determine the process and systems of the household. These systems must be communicated to your children. Parents must retake responsibility for the outcome of their child's education. While a school is there to supply curriculum, the parent is a child's primary educator. It's in parents' prayers and expectations of their children combined with the systematic, disciplined approach to help them reach success that fuels progress. There must be a goal and a plan to achieve it. After all, children are children, not adults.

Deuteronomy says, "Write these on the posts of your home, tell your children day and night...." (11:20 author's paraphrase). As I've referenced many times so far, parents are instructed to teach their children morning, noon, and night.

I believe in a Christian education. In my opinion, the spiritual and educational cannot be separated, but as a parent who wants his or her child to excel, to go further in life, education, and experience than you, it is your God-given job to teach him or her morning, noon, and night all day, every day. Parents teach by example, with words, expectations, discipline, and holding the child accountable to enable them to achieve excellence in all they do.

Competence is within every child's reach, and the future of our families, our nation, is in the hands of our parents. Parents' expectations of their children and personal examples are the primary determiners of success. While this does not happen 100 percent of the time, statistics bear witness that students succeed when parents are involved.

To turn the tide we must—we *must*—change our paradigm. Each sector of our society must accept responsibility for their student influence. Each sector must purposefully influence students to reach whole competence. From leadership and character competence to academic competence, each sector has a role to play and must play to win. Education must be reengineered so our best team is on the field.

At our 2020 t.Lab Black Tie Gala, t.Lab parent, Attorney Pamela Parrish, shared the critical need for involved parenting and the success realized from generation to generation. Attorney Parrish's is a message for all parents:

> As parents our responsibility is to be a bridge from the rich legacy of our ancestors to the journey we hope and dream for our children. When our children are young, they cannot be expected to have the necessary perspective and vision. That is our job as parents.
>
> And it's been my experience that the window of opportunity to make a difference in our children's lives goes by so fast—in a flash the elementary, middle school, and high school years are over. And I'm going to say two things now that are perhaps contradictory.
>
> Number one, it is never too late for us to guide our child. But number two, it is better to start as early as you can.
>
> Jay Z put it this way, "Rosa Parks sat so Martin Luther King Jr. could walk. Martin Luther King Jr. walked so Obama could run. Obama ran so we can fly."
>
> Parents are to guide their children in ensuring their students are poised to fly. Parents are to ensure their children are poised to take advantage of the opportunities won by our ancestors.

SUCCESSFUL STUDENTS: A VILLAGE PARADIGM

The truth is children and adults enjoy what they're good at. Why not create competence through diligence in fields that fuel America's progress and global competitiveness? Instead of focusing only on what the child wants to do at the moment, focus on their future success.

Parents, educators, and all mentors must compel students to pursue the career training and jobs of the future. Doors will open to any career a student is prepared to enter.

Unfortunately, this is not the path many parents or educators tread with their students today. Many, if not most, students' interests change as they grow and learn, which means their career interests shift. Competence, though, will continually produce self-confidence and will open doors of opportunity as high school students diligently build competence that forms a competitive college application. Exploration of career choices should not be limited. Careers in technology, health care, and engineering—even hybrid careers that combine elements of these fields of study—will continue to build the future and are critically needed today because of our global marketplace. A first-class education in needed fields combined with a character education will lead today's generation into the future.

Today's IT jobs, high-level IT positions—software design, creation, and development— and other functions are performed by non-American employees who often do not live within our borders. It is becoming more and more common for a US-based company to manage a team or teams of Indian IT executives and professionals. Why? Because these countries know the need and encourage their children to engage in these fields.

Medicine and technology are just two examples where jobs will grow and will support families. The competencies required to fill those jobs are changing rapidly, and by preparing our students for STEM advancements we are both providing for their future families as well as the security of our nation.

This began in the '80s and '90s. I saw it firsthand at Chrysler Company. In short, employees of domestic companies living abroad in foreign countries are beginning to dominate the American workforce. These employees are sometimes more qualified and committed because they see the opportunity in America. Why aren't Americans seeing and filling those opportunities? Because not enough American children are educated and prepared with the competence to even see the opportunity.

For example, in South Korea, the standard expectation for students to participate in *hagwon* academies which, like t.Lab, are after-school programs for educational excellence. As a result, by age fifteen, each South Korean student has 6.9 years *more formal education* than the American counterpart. The mountain of religion supports this with a night of prayer for their students prior to the national test date.

In this way, our village needs to understand that the future will be different than the past, that old paradigms no longer work. The jobs of today and tomorrow are not the jobs of yesterday. We must pint our students to desire success in careers newly available.

The old ways of "doing things" is outdated in our technology-rich culture. Our culture is very different today than it was even a decade ago. It is time to embrace the shifts we see in technology, in where and how we learn, and use these to develop whole competence in our students.

TRAINING PARENTS FOR EXCELLENCE

Educating parents about the importance of spiritually based and practical curricula is essential for academic excellence among their children. With the right training, parents can become instigators of wisdom in their households, teaching not only skills related to knowledge but also emotional maturity. By acknowledging and addressing the spiritual aspect of a student's education, parents are better equipped to give their children the tools needed to excel academically and live a fulfilled life. The curriculum should focus on topics such as mindfulness, resilience, compassion, and intro-spection—all valuable skills for navigating the world.

Beyond the spiritual aspect, providing parents with practical training is also key in helping students reach academic excellence. This can include strategies for tackling difficult subjects, time man-agement techniques, and tips on how to keep focus in the face of distractions. All these skills are essential for students to thrive academically, and parents need to know that they have a role in helping their children develop them.

Ultimately, providing parents with training that is spiritually based and practical can help them become better mentors and guides to their children. By teaching the importance of wisdom, emotional maturity, and practical skills, they can open a whole world of possibilities for their kids. With the right training, parents will be able to cultivate an environment that promotes academic excellence—one that is both spiritually enriching and academically rewarding. With the right guidance, students can go beyond just passing their classes to become agents of positive transformation in the world.

Raising children is a challenging but rewarding experience. As parents, we must find ways to help our children develop spiritually, morally, and ethically. The Bible is full of tools that can be used to guide our children on their path towards excellence.

KEYS FOR EXCELLENCE

Earlier, I've cited Bishop Ben Gibert. He has created useful keys for parents who want to train excellence into their children.

Opportunity of spiritual empowerment—God will help you. When you don't feel like you're getting it, pray.

You know how many kids are trying to learn without the Holy Spirit? And the Bible says the Holy Spirit teaches, so you've got to teach them that God will help, and yes I can help you, the tutor can help you, mentor can inspire you, teach you—God will help you. God will teach you.

Emphasis of repetition: I already know that; I already did that; I've already learned that; I don't need to do that again. You know what that leads to? That leads to holes in your foundational learning. You got to get the kids understand repetition is a good thing. My flash card to my daughter when she was much younger, she's like "I've already seen that one" I said "yes, but can you do it? Seven times seven? if you're using your fingers we need done it enough times." Don't be like most church members—you kickoff something, you use the same scripture, they assume they know what you're going to talk about, they start to look at each other (...) If I'm teaching the same thing I taught two years ago, unless you walked in (...) you need to hear it again. Paul wrote to Timothy, he said this is how (...), this is how I tell that you're a good minister—that you teach the foundational principles with repetition. Repetition is good, they've been (...) again because you are going to need it for the rest of your life. One of my daughters asked my wife Charisse about Algebra. She's good in Math but you know I am an engineer, so I live by Math. So Dr. C was like, "I don't think I've known how to do this. This is three unknowns. Why don't you ask your dad?" They were all like, "Dad's forgotten all of that." They thought I was too old to do it so I took the challenge. Not only did I do it, I made it look hard. "So this is three places, three unknowns. Let me show you the matrix method."

Exposure to the Global, Giftings, God Variety, and Excellence. Those are four different things. They need to be exposed to some global things. I'm not saying you got to take them to Shanghai and everything but make sure they have a sense of the world—that the world is big and really need to understand that. As language barriers come down, distance barriers come down—and they're really down—they're going to have to compete at least on a global level. In other words, locally, with an eye towards what people can do everywhere.

Giftings—that should be a discussion point in your house, not every day but sometimes. What are you anointed to do? What are you gifted to do? What are you good at? You can just say to that but it's more important that they understand the giftings part because what you're gifted to do, what you have a proclivity for, the anointing will increase just by your submission and fear of the Lord. If you're good at that, when you pray, it's getting better. It's not just your exercise, it's you're empowering. It's very important to understand that. I can get better in some things just by spending 45 minutes in prayer. There are some times I (...) "you know, that was a new way of thinking about that. Where'd you get that from? A book?" "Nope." "Going to a conference?" "No, it's something I'm already strong at so I just spent some time praying and the Holy Spirit gave me a new way of looking at it."

God variety—They need to see God variety. As much as you can, expose them to different people that do the things that they're gifted to do so they can see different administrations and applications of it. So they don't get in a pigeonhole box, it has to look like this.

Excellence—Expose them to excellence, things that are done well, things that are done striving to be, you know—that's why I really apologize for being late, that's a bad example for the kids—but even we go feel crazy period we go back and figure out how do we function in a period like this so that this ever happens again we know how to do it.

And then guard against the attacks of this generation. I gave you the nine attacks; you may want to look at that list, you want to guard against that—that'll mess up your kids. One I really feel the focus on now is Destiny Delays. Watch destiny delays—watch it when your kids are not progressing educationally, empowerment wise, not working. Josh just got out of school, he's got a film degree from the University of Michigan, and I didn't have to tell you: we celebrated for about four days. After four days he's like, "Well, here's my plan: I'm already working into church, I'm really interested in helping with the announcements, get some video and stuff, social media. I got a one-hour internship then I've got three options associated with that—I should have that done by September. I'm going to make a decision on whether I'm going to work for a company here, I'm going to go to New York, I'm going to go to California. I'm going to talk to you about that and I will make that decision by September 15. I plan on being deployed by October. I'm just going to be here this time." I was like, "That's okay, no problem." Because he needed to take an off because college was so rough.

Recognize the opportunity and urgency. Everybody says 7, 13, 18, 21, and 30. 18 and 21 transitional years between teen and adult, it doesn't happen like that. They've studied brainwaves now and they know 18, 19 to 21 and then go into 26th the way the brainwaves work shifts. Stuff that they could do, they couldn't do, they can now do. Some stuff that was really difficult at 14 you should tell them to try it again at 18. The one who wasn't good at Math then try this now because they can actually get better; their brainwaves actually changed in a way. Between 21 and 30, you really ought to be honing in. You don't have to know exactly what you're going to be and what you're going to do but you need to know what your giftings are, and you're working in it or getting educated in it. Because by the time you're 30, you should have a resume and capability that somebody looks and says, "Oh you can do that?" You can sell; you can build—does that make sense?

THE BIBLE AND EXCELLENCE OF WISDOM
From the book of Proverbs, we are encouraged to "Train up a child in the way he should go: and when he is old, he will not depart from it" (Proverbs 22:6 KJV). This Scripture reminds us that our children's spiritual foundation must be established early on so

that they may remain rooted in the knowledge of the Lord for life. Additionally, Proverbs 3:5–6 reads, "Trust in the Lord with all your heart and lean not on your own understanding; in all your ways acknowledge him, and he will make your paths straight." This is a reminder for us to remain humble and obedient to God's teachings so that our children may do the same.

We must also ensure that our children are equipped with wisdom in order to make sound decisions. Ecclesiastes 7:12 states, "Wisdom is a shelter as money is a shelter, but the advantage of knowledge is this: Wisdom preserves those who have it." We can use this Scripture to instill in our children that wisdom and knowledge are essential components for living an abundant life.

Finally, we must remember that obedience is the key to success. Deuteronomy 11:26–28 reads, "See, I am setting before you today a blessing and a curse—the blessing if you obey the commands of the Lord your God that I am giving you today; the curse if you disobey the commands of the Lord your God and turn from the way that I command you today." This Scripture reminds us to be obedient to our heavenly Father's teachings so that we may live a life filled with blessings.

Raising children is an important responsibility for parents. With the help of the Scriptures and tools of the Bible, we can ensure that our children build a strong foundation of faith, wisdom, and obedience for a life of excellence.

Raising children according to the Bible should be a paramount goal for any parent or guardian. It's not only about obedience and following the rules; it's about raising children with excellence and wisdom. Deuteronomy 6:6–9 (NKJV) outlines this concept perfectly: "And these words which I command you today shall be in your heart... You shall teach them diligently to your children, and shall talk of them when you sit in your house, when you walk by the way, when you lie down, and when you rise up." In these verses we are instructed to instill God's wisdom into our children through consistent teaching and showing them examples of obedience.

This is a tall order, but with faith and dedication, every parent can help their children grow in excellence and wisdom. As Dr. Martin Luther King Jr. once said: "Intelligence plus character—that is the goal of true education. The complete education gives one not only power of concentration, but worthy objectives upon which to concentrate." By establishing the Bible as our manual for raising children, we can impart both knowledge and character into their lives for generations to come.

It is up to us to teach our children the importance of obedience in their everyday lives, and help them become examples of excellence and wisdom. By doing so, we are fulfilling God's command in Deuteronomy 6:6–9 and ensuring our children are equipped to lead a life of purpose and meaning.

The Bible, with its timeless wisdom, is the manual all parents should use when raising their children. Through diligent teaching, thoughtful examples, and unwavering faith, we can help equip the next generation for success.

Today, more than ever before, we must work to pass the knowledge of God's Word down to our children and ensure they are learning how to live in excellence and wisdom. It is only with true education—with intelligence plus character—that we can lead our families into a brighter tomorrow. With faith and dedication, we can fulfill God's command to teach our children diligently and help them live a life of purpose and meaning.

The Bible is the manual to which all parents should look when raising their families—a timeless source of wisdom that will equip our children for success in this world, and the next. Let us take up

Deuteronomy 6:6-9 and teach our children diligently, so that they may know how to live in excellence and wisdom.

By doing this, we are making sure that the next generation is equipped not just with knowledge and power of concentration, but with the worthy objective of obedience to God's Word. This is the foundation of true education, and it is the only way to pass down timeless wisdom from one generation to the next. Let us take up this challenge together and establish the Bible as our manual for raising children. When we do so with faith, dedication, and love, we can help ensure our families will live in excellence and wisdom for generations to come.

As a leader, I believe that the Bible is the ultimate manual for raising children. In particular, Deuteronomy 6:6–9 provides invaluable wisdom and guidance for guiding our little ones towards academic excellence and strong character. The passage clearly explains to us parents that we should take every opportunity to teach our kids the laws of God so they can eventually live a life of obedience and faith.

This is where I believe the greatest challenge lies—teaching children to strive for excellence in academics, while also instilling within them a moral compass that guides their decisions and actions. As adults, we must remain mindful of our role as parents by ensuring that our children develop meaningful relationships with the Lord. We must also be intentional in our teachings, helping them to understand that obedience is essential for success.

One of the best ways to ensure academic excellence and character are intertwined is by providing examples through stories and experiences. For instance, when your child has done well on an assignment or project, take a moment to share with them how God has provided them with the wisdom and strength to succeed. Similarly, when your child falters or does something wrong, use it as an opportunity to teach them an important lesson about obedience and humility.

Overall, Deuteronomy 6:6–9 provides us parents with a valuable reminder of how vital it is that we use our time wisely and intentionally to raise our children in the way of the Lord. By teaching them to strive for excellence academically as well as towards growing in character, we will be leading them into a life of potential and promise that's rooted firmly in faith. As Dr. Martin Luther King Jr. said, "Intelligence plus character—that is the goal of true education." By using God's Word as our guide, we can help equip our children and their futures with both knowledge and character.

THE AFRICAN AMERICAN TEAM APPROACH

Every generation of African Americans has borne a collective responsibility to make sure that our children seek access to and receive a quality education. If we are going to move forward as a community, it is essential that we assemble and deploy the brightest and best professionals—teachers, administrators, counselors, coaches, and support staff—to transform education within our community in order to ensure that our children are equipped with the skills, knowledge, and confidence to compete in a globalized economy.

We must reject mediocrity and political incompetence in how education is conducted and administered within the African American community. We cannot accept substandard performance; we must challenge ourselves and strive for excellence with the existing educational resources. Our students must be able to use them because of character and determination. We must be bold in our commitment to the transformation of education for African American students, both within our communities and around the world.

In this effort, we must equip our children with the skills needed to succeed in a rapidly changing global economy—the ability to think critically, communicate effectively, and solve problems collaboratively. We must provide them with the tools to become responsible and contributing citizens, instilling in them a sense of purpose and a commitment to helping others. We must ensure that no child is left behind, regardless of race or economic status.

It is our responsibility to create an educational system within the African American community that will enable our children—and generations to come—to compete on an equal footing with their peers around the world. We must strive to make sure that each and every African American child has access to a quality education, including the same level of resources available to those in other communities. Together, we can create an educational system that will provide our children with the tools and skills they need for success, putting them on a path to global competitiveness.

When we come together in this way, we can be sure that the transformation of education within our community will lead us to a brighter future. It is essential that every African American join together in this effort and do their part to ensure the success of our children's educational future. Together, we can achieve excellence.

FOUR FACTORS FOR THE BEST AFRICAN AMERICAN TEAM ON THE FIELD

In order for African American communities to put the best team on the field through education, four factors must be in place: adequate organizations and systems to allocate resources; committed leaders with vision united by a common set of goals and metrics; measurements to effectively measure the academic competence of students; and highly competitive yet cooperative organizations that foster excellence.

First, without proper systems and organizational structure to allocate resources and drive a common agenda, African American educational attainment lags far behind other student populations. Without proper funding and organizational structure, educational attainment lags far behind that of other student populations.

Second, African American communities need committed leaders with vision united by a common set of goals and metrics. These leaders must have the courage to create a clear vision for educational success, as well as the necessary organizational skills to ensure that resources are allocated effectively.

Third, it is essential to have a common set of metrics to measure academic competence. This helps identify areas where students may need additional support or direction, enabling educators and community members to work together to meet the needs of students.

Appendix One contains a chart of the competence measurement systems used in our society with recent score trends. Those who argue with these standard requirements are at heart contending against our own students' competence. As Dr. King described, the most dangerous things are sincere ignorance and conscientious stupidity, producing the same result. Dr. King would predict these conditions for any education systems without standard measurements for competence.

Finally, African American communities should strive for highly competitive yet cooperative organizations that foster excellence. Splinter groups and political divisions can lead to confusion and incompetence, thus lowering academic standards in the classroom. By cultivating a spirit of collaboration and competition within organizations, an environment where competency and excellence can be encouraged is created, leading to greater educational attainment.

In conclusion, African American communities have the potential to establish strong educational systems that will set students up for success in the future. To do this, they must address four key factors: adequate organizations and systems to allocate resources; committed leaders with vision united by a common set of goals and metrics; measurements to effectively measure the academic competence of students; and highly competitive yet cooperative organizations that foster excellence. By addressing these factors, African American communities can ensure that the best teams are put on the field for educational attainment.

THE BEST TEAM PARADIGM

Should only the wealthiest with the most advantages or those with the highest intelligence rankings among us expect excellence from their children? Of course not. In fact, Malcolm Gladwell's book *David and Goliath* includes a story of a wealthy Hollywood executive who believes the opposite. Children from the wealthiest families face disadvantages, such as keeping up or surpassing their parents' level of success. According to this wealthy executive the middle is probably the best place to be.

Biblically, parents bear the responsibility. I'm often amazed at parents who sit back and allow a child to make a decision they are not capable of making. Every three months we complete a performance review of each t.Lab student, and often guide parents in helping their children mature faster because the demands of life command this to happen, but it doesn't always happen.

Parents must be aware and diligent—every day. To use a Tiger Woods term, parents have to be on their "A-game" every day. If they are not, they will lose an opportunity to guide and influence their children in important moments.

I'm always surprised at the large number of parents who decided to raise their children differently than how they were raised. Parents of baby boomers were prescriptive with their children. In contrast, many parents today allow their children to choose their career without any type of guidance or insight. I believe that's a mistake. Many of my peers even push back at me, "Well, who are you to tell me what to do. Can't they make a decision?"

Often my response is, "Did you teach them how to make a decision?"

"Well, no."

"Then how do you expect them to decide?"

Expecting a young student to possess the wisdom to choose their path is more often than not overreaching. Most college students change their career choice. In fact, some statistics indicate 80 percent of college students change their major at least once, which often adds to the already high cost of college.

Students need someone to nudge them, to push them. That's a part of the parenting process. The first and most critical component of success is identity. Each child should know his or her worth is derived from God, our Creator. Then parents should teach their children to make sound decisions.

Parents must wake up every day renewed in their responsibility. The first words parents speak every morning should be "Lord, grant me wisdom, patience, and insight to guide this child." Just that simple confession will help parents lead their children. God will provide everything parents need to lead their children down the right path.

That said, the current drivers of education must change. There is a need today for a radical shift in paradigm on the part of parents, teachers, *and leaders* in order for education to produce competent graduates ready to solve today's problems and create tomorrow's successes.

STUDENT WINS IT ALL – AIM PROGRAM PRODUCES RESULTS FOR STEM MAJORS

A friend and t.Lab family has two sons in t.Lab. He and I are of different races and have differing views on some things, yet we respect each another and get along fine. His son began our program in the third grade. Fourteen years later, he is one of our best students at the postsecondary level.

The father and I have differing opinions on some matters. If I were the type of person who hears what people say instead of watching what they do, I could have been offended many times due to his differing opinions on most matters. Our friendship soars, however. Today, that father will tell you t.Lab is a reason his son has been able to excel and to rise.

This young man is competitive; he is a great student. Since third grade he listened to speeches about attending Kettering University's summer STEM program before his twelfth-grade year began, alongside his fellow t.Lab students. Kettering is one of the most expensive colleges in Michigan, and the school developed a program to boost minority admissions twenty years ago, which includes a summer STEM competition for rising seniors over a five-week period, competing in chemistry, physics, biology, and other subjects.

My friend, the student's father, will tell you that t.Lab is one reason this student has been able to excel. The summer program winner receives a full-tuition scholarship to the university. Kettering has built a pipeline of minority students and today is one of the only universities in America where students of color compete with the highest GPAs.

This student grew up listening to this story while participating in t.Lab, a program designed for academic excellence in spite of a student's ethnicity. He expected to go to Kettering's summer program. There was no way I could tell him that he couldn't go. Thankfully, he was able to receive minority status and benefit from t.Lab's long-time relationship with the university.

How could I have not allowed him to compete in this program? How could I have remained ethical and moral and tell him that he couldn't participate with his fellow t.Lab students because of his race? I just kept telling him the same story I told everyone else.

This student went, and he won. He became t.Lab's first ever Kettering's AIM first place winner. When I told his father he won, his response was, "Of course he did. He did mostly everything you requested him to do."

THE BEST TEAM, NOW

These days, experience, insight, and expertise proven through results in any industry are not always the requirements of our leaders. Technology makes it possible for anyone to have a voice. Unfortunately, the voices we hear are not always the voices that have a proven track record of results. Moving forward, we must choose educational leaders, even consider leaders from the outside, that understand the crisis of competence we are facing. Such leaders are committed to correcting the issue, and have a proven track record of developing and maintaining programs proven to consistently deliver competence.

Change must happen now. Our international neighbors are utilizing and leveraging the technologies we created and provided them to outperform us in many areas. Make no mistake, America is faltering and no longer ahead of our neighbors in education. Yet other countries have the vision and the tools to grow and excel. Combine their vision with the financial resources necessary to achieve it, and they are gaining ground.

America needs a new vision. Our competitors are playing to win, and so should we. To win, to rise, we must put our best team on the field.

But what happens if we don't?

CHAPTER 9

WHAT WILL HAPPEN IF WE DO NOT CHANGE?

While it has been said that our economy may be eclipsed by China, they haven't surpassed us yet. America continues to lead the world in Gross Domestic Product (GDP). America is known for innovation, and today China is capitalizing on American innovation from the 80s, 90s, and 2000s. The power of American intellect, innovation, and entrepreneurship provided China the tools and the knowledge necessary to innovate and change—let's be fact-based.

America must innovate once more to lead globally. The solutions to the problems of today and tomorrow already exist within our students. Our job is to give them the educational competence that allows our students to develop them.

America has elevated the world through innovation, but now, our country faces threats to our continued global leadership. We must ensure that our innovation continues, following examples such as Dr. Bill Pickard, Attorney John Daniels, Rosalind Brewer, Dr. Hobart Harris, Dr. Darnell Kailger, David Steward, Mellody Hobson Lucas, Robert F. Smith, David Tarver, and Carla Harris.

Like these leaders, we must embrace innovation and value ingenuity fueled by academic competence. Our ability to envision tomorrow combined with the knowledge and ability to create it will help us reach Mars before other countries. It will enable us to use the moon and its resources, create vaccines needed now and in the future, and cure cancer.

The will to innovate can solve our social problems. We can be an America that leads the world. We must again focus on exporting our new culture and values, including sports and entertainment. Innovation can enable us to create a country and a civilization that values all. Our citizens can embrace equality among all ethnic groups and genders, and defend freedom of religion. We must educate tomorrow's pastors and shepherds. To get there we need an effective, first-class education system.

A LONG WARNING, MORE URGENT

The warning bell was rung in 1981 when T. H. Bell, the US Secretary of Education during the Reagan administration, formed the National Commission on Excellence in Education and requested a report on the quality of education in America be completed by April 1983.

Interestingly, the report, titled *A Nation at Risk: The Imperative for Educational Reform*, reported revealed findings that include many of the same issues we face today. Here is a glance at some of the 1983 report findings:

> International comparisons of student achievement, completed a decade ago, reveal that on 19 academic tests American students were never first or second and, in comparison with other industrialized nations, were last seven times.

> Average achievement of high school students on most standardized tests is now lower than when Sputnik was launched.

Over half the population of gifted students do not match their tested ability with comparable achievement in school.

The College Board's Scholastic Aptitude Tests (SAT) demonstrate a virtually unbroken decline from 1963 to 1980. Average verbal scores fell over 50 points and average mathematics scores dropped nearly 40 points.

College Board achievement tests also reveal consistent declines in recent years in such subjects as physics and English.

Both the number and proportion of students demonstrating superior achievement on the SATs (i.e., those with scores of 650 or higher) have also dramatically declined.

Between 1975 and 1980, remedial mathematics courses in public four-year colleges increased by 72 percent and now constitute one-quarter of all mathematics courses taught in those institutions.

Average tested achievement of students graduating from college is also lower.

Business and military leaders complain that they are required to spend millions of dollars on costly remedial education and training programs in such basic skills as reading, writing, spelling, and computation. The Department of the Navy, for example, reported to the Commission that one-quarter of its recent recruits cannot read at the ninth-grade level, the minimum needed simply to understand written safety instructions. Without remedial work they cannot even begin, much less complete, the sophisticated training essential in much of the modern military.

[Source: https://edreform.com/wp-content/uploads/2013/02/
A_Nation_At_Risk_1983.pdf]

The report identifies why these 1983 findings were alarming. These deficiencies come at a time when the demand for highly skilled workers in new fields is accelerating rapidly. For example:

Computers and computer-controlled equipment are penetrating every aspect of our lives—homes, factories, and offices.

One estimate indicates that by the turn of the century millions of jobs will involve laser technology and robotics.

Technology is radically transforming a host of other occupations. They include health care, medical science, energy production, food processing, construction, and the building, repair, and maintenance of sophisticated scientific, educational, military, and industrial equipment.

A Nation at Risk revealed America was experiencing "a rising tide of mediocrity that threatens our very future as a nation and a people." This tide of mediocrity has at the very least continued over the four decades since the 1983 report. We have remained the largest economy on the planet and technology innovators aided America's continued success, but we now face similar threats because of our growing lack of educational competence.

Fast-forward to 2020. In February 2020, Elon Musk said, "A thing that will feel pretty strange is that the Chinese economy is probably going to be at least twice as big as the United States economy, maybe three times," during a conversation with Air Force Lt. General John Thompson at the Air Warfare Symposium in Orlando, Florida. [https://www.cnbc.com/2020/02/28/musk-says-chinese-economy-will-surpass-the-us-by-two-or-three-times.html]

Musk then added, "The foundation of war is economics. If you have half the resources of the counterparty then you better be real innovative. If you're not innovative, you're going to lose." This idea of innovation fueling competition is a challenge today's students *must* embrace in order to take the US into the future secure economically and militarily.

A nation's population size as related to political force will hurt America if we do not change. America's uncertain future rests in the hands of our children's competence. Our children today are the fuel for tomorrow's economy and innovation. With a new paradigm, we can unleash the potential of our entire population, including African Americans, and simultaneously provide equity through the power of intellect, competence, character, and innovation.

NOW IS TIME FOR A PARADIGM SHIFT

If China goes to Mars before the US, where does this leave us? Behind. Behind in technology means behind in defense and behind in the creation of tomorrow's technology. Without continued American innovation fueled by educational competence we could become the consumers of other countries' technological excellence, not the creators. Why? Because these countries build competence in math and science early. Their children are good at it.

If you need an example, consider the TikTok sale. To protect Americans' privacy, the government decided to ban the social media platform if an American company did not purchase it from a Chinese company. And China's threat does not end there. There are reports they are using AI to collect our information and even

DNA to sell us health care in the future. Add to that China's imperialistic tendencies today.

It is time for a radical paradigm shift. It is time for a shift of perspective on the part of parents and all involved in education that results in America again expecting diligence on the part of students that leads our country to remaining the producer at the forefront of the world. Our children have great minds but their competence for their own patents has suffered. We must educate our students in such a way that they reach their capability.

Think about this: If your child is good at something, and diligence creates competence in whatever they undertake, they will enjoy it. Children, and adults for that matter, enjoy what they're good at.

Our legacy, America's future, is at stake, and while parents play the most critical role, educational leaders from teachers, mentors, and coaches to heads of schools and government entities have a critical role to play as well. African American students must be drafted into the innovation wars and equipped to succeed in them. Each generation should aspire to do better than the preceding one. This is biblical, but this is not where we are in America right now. This is not happening with American students today, especially with African Americans. Asian Americans are performing the best. So where does this leave us as a nation? Jobs today are global, which means our students must be the best in order to be competitive for jobs at home in America or across the globe.

POOR EDUCATION ERODES THE OTHER SIX SPHERES

The Mountain of Education is a crucial component of any society, and its importance cannot be overstated. Its influence can be seen in the other six Mountains of Influence—Economic Opportunity, Political Power, Social Standing, Health and Wellness, Morality and Ethics, Spiritual Faith—all of which are necessary for a civilization to flourish. When this mountain is neglected, it creates a ripple effect that can be felt throughout the entire system.

For example, if the quality of education provided in a society is poor, this has an immediate and direct impact on economic opportunity. The citizens of such a society would be ill-equipped to compete for higher-paying positions due to their lack of knowledge, skills, and experience. This lack of competitiveness leads to a decrease in economic opportunity for all involved.

Similarly, the poor quality of education impacts political power. Such citizens would be unable to fully comprehend or analyze issues such as policy, taxation, or regulation due to their low levels of knowledge and understanding. As a result, they are less likely to be involved in political activities, which leads to a weakened voice and reduced influence.

In terms of social standing, those with poor educational backgrounds are much more likely to experience discrimination and prejudice due to their limited knowledge. This can lead to feelings of inferiority or worthlessness, which further exacerbates an already existing social divide.

The poor Mountain of Education also affects health and wellness. Without knowledge of proper diet, hygiene, and preventive healthcare, citizens are more prone to illness or injury due to inadequate care. This can lead to long-term physical or mental impairments that can further hinder a person's prospects in life.

Likewise, when the educational level of a society is low, morality and ethics can suffer. Without knowledge of right and wrong, citizens are more likely to engage in unethical or immoral behavior which can have a serious impact on the overall quality of life.

Finally, spiritual faith may be diminished when the Mountain of Education is neglected. Without adequate education, it becomes difficult for citizens to properly understand and appreciate the power of their faith, which can lead to a decline in religious participation.

In conclusion, the Mountain of Education is essential for the success of any society. Without quality education, all other Mountains of Influence suffer, leading to reduced economic opportunity, weakened political power, decreased social standing, poorer health and wellness, decreased morality and ethics, and a lack of spiritual faith. It is therefore paramount that this mountain be given the proper attention and investment to ensure a successful future.

IT'S BEEN DONE BEFORE

Earlier I cited the warning of Dr. Claude Anderson that a sector of the African American community risk becoming a permanent underclass due to poor education and other systemic factors.

This risk is not limited; the same is true of Americans of all races. If our country's education does not produce competence, there will be war of many kinds. Our students will suffer diminished lives under the limits of their diminished competence, and our country will lack the collective character to compete and survive on the world stage.

But it need not end this way. Dr. James D. Anderson's writing, cited earlier, shows that against every imaginable obstacle, the African American community put their best team on the field. Dr. Martin Luther King Jr. is one of many exemplary leaders produced by their efforts.

It's been done before, and it can be done again. The sphere of education is essential for the success of any society. Without quality education, all other spheres of society suffer, leading to reduced economic opportunity, weakened political power, decreased social standing, poorer health and wellness, decreased morality and ethics, and a lack of spiritual faith. It is therefore paramount that this sphere be given the proper attention and investment to ensure a successful future.

Transformation is required—in educators, in our systems, in our national priorities. Engaged in the process must be technology and culture alike, with a common mission to unleash our students' potential and establish a multi-generational legacy.

Without such a transformation of the US educational system, we will grow weaker and suffer for it as a nation.

CHAPTER 10

TRANSFORMATION, AN APPROACH TO DRIVE CHANGE

THE T-LAB SYSTEM CONSISTENTLY DELIVERS COMPETENCE

Challenges abound for parents, educators, and educational leaders to enable students to reach academic excellence, yet it is critical we do so. t.Lab understands these realities. All the factors we see in society that can distract from the goal of our students reaching competence must be challenged by parents, educators, and leaders if our children are to reach their potential.

The goal of independent and self-directed learners can be difficult for students who are less mature. That is why we focus on character development and emotional intelligence. Parents must be on their "A-game" every single day, to use a phrase Tiger Woods coined. If a parent is not diligent, an opportunity to guide and direct and influence their child in the proper way could be missed.

t.Lab is only part of a student's education. I am not suggesting our program is the only solution. We are effective because we do not replace traditional school; we leverage Common Core curriculum and expect that students reach competence through diligence and rigor. This is true for all top 1 percent academic performers. The skills and subjects tested on the standardized tests are taught throughout America's education system today. t.Lab instruction combined with traditional school work together to ensure a student achieves competence. We are a niche highlighting the need for a serious conversation that needs to occur between educational leaders from government, business, schools, and programs like ours, to create a system of education that consistently delivers results, as measured by competence.

INCREASING A STUDENT'S ACT SCORE

The challenge of increasing an ACT score from 28 to 35 is immense due to the large standard deviation between these two points. It requires a deep understanding of how the ACT works, significant effort and dedication, and often external support in order to succeed. Without adequate institutional resources or access to expert guidance, it can be nearly impossible to bridge this gap.

The challenge is far less difficult when trying to increase a score from 16.1 to 21.25, as this requires only minor improvements in core competencies rather than significant changes and growth. This makes it easier for individuals to reach the next level of excellence with their ACT scores.

While effort and dedication are essential elements of success on the ACT, character also plays an important role. An individual's commitment to self-improvement and drive to reach higher levels of excellence can be just as influential as their knowledge of the material and test-taking skills. Ultimately, it is a combination of these factors that will enable someone to increase their composite score from 28 to 35 in spite of a lack of institutional support. It is possible, but requires significant dedication and determination. With the right attitude and commitment to self-improvement, anything is possible.

By understanding the challenges, recognizing what it takes to excel, and demonstrating a level of character that is admirable and inspirational, anyone can increase their ACT score from 28 to 35. It may be difficult; but with the right attitude and dedication to self-improvement, anything is possible. With a commitment to excellence and competence in core competencies, it is possible to achieve the goal of a 35 composite score. The challenge is well worth the effort and reward.

DILIGENCE PRODUCES SCORE IMPROVEMENT

One local parent was a single mother whose daughter has been in t.Lab since third grade and is now in college. Undoubtedly, single parenting comes with challenges. This mother works a lot, so over the years I have sat in for her during the weekly meeting which t.Lab conducts with each student and parent. Because of my presence, I've seen firsthand the development of this student. She was not meeting t.Lab benchmarks as a sophomore because she was not following through with her weekly tasks. Her composite ACT score would fluctuate on practice tests. Her competence in Microsoft Suite and Bloomberg Business Markets Concepts developed slowly.

At the end of eleventh grade, and before attending Kettering University's AIM Pre-College Program, this young lady realized the Microsoft Specialist Certification in MS Word and MS PowerPoint. She also received her score on the February 2019 ACT. A different t.Lab student who took the ACT at the same time received a 17. Comparing that score with her own, the young lady saw what a difference her diligence made. She called me with excitement in her voice, obviously happy, and shared that she received a composite score of 28 on ACT. We celebrated her achievement.

Her 28 on the ACT placed her in the top 10 percent of all students in the nation. "I could get a 36," she said, now even more committed. She recognized the value of all we had been encouraging her to do.

This and the many other testimonies have convinced me that our model, when followed consistently, produces excellence. Standard deviation for the ACT is 2.5 plus or minus. That means every student who retakes the exam will either increase or decrease by 2.5 points. And our students always move beyond standard deviation positively. These are the results we see occurring.

It's not perfect. Not every student and/or not every parent does what we tell them to do.

But it is all about where and how you spend your time. This I know: if I can get you to spend your time here on this side and be focused, it's much better than being over on the other side, doing nothing.

DILIGENCE PRODUCES COLLEGE SUCCESS

The transformation of this young lady from a student in the top 10% to one of the top 1% in her highly rigorous and competitive university was remarkable. It wasn't merely a product of increased diligence, although that certainly played a role; rather, it required a radical change in her character—spiritually, mentally, and emotionally.

As a high school student, she was content with her place in the top 10%. She enjoyed the relative comfort of academic success without having to push herself too hard. But as she learned more about her chosen field—biochemistry—her eyes were opened to a whole new level of excellence that she had never imagined before. That's when the transformation truly began.

Through the collaboration of faculty and staff, it became evident to her that excellence would no longer consist simply of doing her homework; it would require all of her spiritual, mental, and emotional faculties to be at their peak performance. She dedicated herself to a rigorous daily practice of prayer in order to stay focused on the task at hand. In addition, she diligently studied and executed her classroom assignments with vigor, as well as any extra projects that would help deepen her understanding of the subject.

In the end, the proud student's transformation from a student in the top 10% to the top 1% resulted from her own commitment to excellence and spiritual growth. She also realized a 4.0 GPA. Her hard work and dedication truly paid off, upon her admission into biochemistry, the most difficult curriculum at Kettering University. She is a shining example of what can happen when one is willing to push themselves and strive for excellence in all areas of their life.

Her inspiring story will surely motivate anyone looking to make a similar transformation. With dedication, hard work, and an openness to spiritual growth, anything is possible. Her example proves that excellence can be achieved through diligence and perseverance, with faith in oneself and the courage to make a change. Change is possible; all it takes is the will to succeed.

By following such an example, anyone can strive for greatness and excel in whatever they do. It starts with a commitment to excellence, hard work, and the courage to make a change. This young woman has shown that transformation is within reach and that excellence is achievable. It's up to each person to make the change, and with such results as hers, it's clear that anything is possible with hard work and dedication.

Discipline with diligence creates competence. I see it happen over and over again.

EDUCATION FUELS AMERICA'S CONTINUED SUCCESS

Our student's experience also reflects how well a student will perform in freshman and sophomore years in college. While many argue otherwise, I believe the ACT accurately predicts whether or not a student will perform during the freshman and sophomore years at any given school.

Consider the young woman's progress in her first semester as a freshman at Kettering University. As a biochemistry major, she maintained a 4.0. Kettering's median ACT score of admitted students is a 27, so considering her score of ACT, her success was predictable. The reality is that if a student is within the standard deviation of median score for a university or college, they will likely perform well at that school.

This inspiring young woman is a highly motivated student. All of our students should be highly motivated. If that motivation does not come from an internal drive, their parents and village should be there to help. There is a good reason for our concern.

With these ideals in mind, t.Lab rolled out our Drive to 25 campaign, as discussed earlier. Our goal is to raise the median ACT score of African Americans to 25 by 2025. We feel that by creating academic competence within our communities, we can significantly reduce the impact of some of the current cultural and health issues facing our students. Through our National Advisory Board we expect to reach 250,000 African American students and provide them with t.Lab services especially the two hours of quality tutoring each week by 2025.

Through inference t.Lab is convinced that in elevating ACT scores, in elevating competence, we will change the face of the African American community. We infer raising the median score to 25 will reduce the obesity rate by 15 percent; reduce the number of heart disease related deaths by 5 percent; will reduce the cancer deaths by 5 percent, and in addition will increase incomes, help decrease the percentage of those living in poverty, and will overall change family legacies and therefore communities.

While these numbers will transform the African American community, that is only the start. We also believe teen pregnancy will be reduced by 15 percent and incarcerations will decrease 15 percent too, as will the divorce rate. And t.Lab serves all races and ethnicities. Our goal is ensuring students develop well-rounded competence.

[https://www.usatoday.com/story/news/nation/2013/10/08/literacy-international-workers-education-math-americans/2935909/]

[http://www.oecd.org/pisa/aboutpisa/]

[https://www.npr.org/sections/ed/2016/01/27/464418078/lowering-the-bar-for-the-new-ged-test]

ACCURATE METHODS: EVALUATION AND ASSESSMENT

It is clear that there is a need for more accurate methods to evaluate and assess student performance in academics. The current metrics being used by educational institutions do not adequately reflect the true academic excellence of students or demonstrate their competency level in a way that speaks to their competitiveness.

Graduation rates, graduation levels, hours spent in development sessions, and student feelings on course effectiveness are unreliable indicators of academic competency. These do not measure competency; they measure the output of a failed paradigm.

This problem is further compounded by the trend of large corporations mandating that newly hired college graduates complete third-party tests to validate competency—effectively invalidating the academic achievements previously certified by institutions of higher learning.

This issue should be addressed by leaders in education, who must come together to establish more valid and accurate measures for determining student performance and competency at the secondary and postsecondary levels. These metrics should be data-driven, evidence-based, and reflective of student achievement. By creating a system that accurately reflects the academic excellence of students and their demonstrated competency, educational institutions can ensure that they are preparing students for success in the ever-evolving competitive job market. Furthermore, by developing and implementing a more robust evaluation system, leaders in education will create a better future for students and their communities as a whole.

It is time to put an end to outdated metrics that do not accurately portray student competency levels or adequately prepare them for successful futures. By creating more valid and accurate measures of student performance, educational leaders will be taking a significant step to ensure that students are able to demonstrate their academic excellence and compete at the highest levels. With such an evaluation system in place, students can confidently enter the job market with the assurance that their credentials reflect their true capabilities. It is only through such meaningful reform that students can receive the attention and recognition they deserve for their academic achievements.

CHAPTER 11

COLLEGE CHOICE, MAJOR, AND INCOME

One critical component of higher education is the experience gained by maturing into an adult alongside peers in a learning environment. As high school students transition into independent college students then into college graduates, tremendous maturing is expected to occur.

Scholarly and culturally expanding growth develops a broader worldview, one that creates opportunity not just by the blessing and the degree received, but by the intangibles that come alongside the challenge of learning: self-confidence, knowledge that informs decisions, and an expanding and diverse like-minded adult peer group.

Now add to this mix the importance of college choice. A student who attends a Tier 1 school (generally considered a private, prestigious research institution like Yale or Johns Hopkins) for undergraduate study will earn considerably more than a Tier 2 (selective, private liberal arts colleges like Middlebury and Vassar), Tier 3, and Tier 4 school graduates. "Why You Can't Catch Up," an article in the *New York Times* reveals this disparity, elevating the importance of receiving an undergraduate degree from a top-tier college.

While a male graduate of a Tier 1 college with a graduate degree from a Tier 1 to 3 school earns on average $185,695 a year, a Tier 4 college graduate with a
higher-tier graduate degree earns only $133,236. The
gap for women is even more striking: A Tier 4 college
graduate who attended a higher-tier law school, for
example, earns about 60 percent of the salary of a
lawyer with a B.A. from a Tier 1 college. [https://www.
nytimes.com/2014/08/03/education/edlife/why-you-
cant-catch-up.html]

Consider too the ACT score required to attend a Tier 1 college,
reported in November 2020. The average ACT scores for the
top 38 of the tier 1 schools average ACT scores range from a
perfect 36 (Caltech sits alone here) to a 33 (thirteen of the thir-
ty-eight schools including Emory, Georgetown, Georgia Tech,
and the University of Michigan). [https://blog.prepscholar.com/
colleges-with-highest-act-scores]

Mature teens and young adults who choose not to go to college encounter different experiences, and of course, many challenges that shape and mold them into adults. While some succeed,
most, maybe even almost all of these, are left behind. Here too is
a disparity of income and opportunity. A study from Georgetown
University found that overall on average college graduates earn $1
million more than non-graduates in a lifetime. Pew Research found
college graduates earned about $17,500 more per year than those
who did not graduate from college.

Then there's the income differences between high- and
low-demand majors. Some college students choose majors based
on feelings, not market demand, which places them at an economic disadvantage. It is critical college students embrace the
fields most needed that compensate accordingly. Majors that fuel

high-demand careers pay considerably more. According to the Center for Education and the Workforce at Georgetown University, "The top-paying college majors earn $3.4 million more than the lowest-paying majors over a lifetime." In summary, a student forfeits $1 million by not graduating from college, and a college graduate forfeits $3.4 million for choosing a low-demand major.

Wealth creates opportunity and experiences which a lack of wealth cannot afford. Add to that the statistics revealing a shrinking of middle-class wealth while the wealthiest are gaining wealth at a greater pace than in recent years.

t.Lab educates students on the consequences of college choice while simultaneously working to ready them for a Tier 1 university in STEM disciplines. We encourage and guide them to choose an in-demand field, because the major field of study strongly influences their competence for our society. It also places them in positions to benefit from high demand.

We expect our students to advance by one grade level competency every three months. Our average student joins our program beginning their second grade year. We expect them to be college-ready after their sixth grade year. If a student begins in third grade, that student will have completed their senior year in high school by the end of their eighth grade year. By the time they are in high school they will have a clear advantage on the ACT (and SAT) and the foundation necessary to help them compete in high school for top spots in their high schools, which leads to college scholarships.

Because college graduates can afford a better life, and college-focused students result in fewer teen pregnancies, lower obesity rates, and less drug use, a significant increase in college graduations will result in a reduction in the issues impacting the poor today. This alone will improve America.

However, not all colleges are equal, and it is important for a student to choose the right college or university. *Fail U* by Charles Sykes reveals the exorbitant cost of a college degree. Since 1978 the cost of a bachelor's degree "has soared 1125 percent since 1978, 4 times the rate of inflation, even as the value of that degree is increasingly questioned." A generation of graduates now "carry a crushing debt burden," according to the author, "but without the skills or job prospects once taken for granted." This increase, according to the *Fail U* author, has occurred even though the degree's value is increasingly questioned.

In addition, college spending on instruction remains flat. The money went to buildings, administration, promotions, athletics, and non-instructional student services. Campuses compete with facilities and multiply the number of administrators. All of this was paid for by student debt.

The outcome of education 2012 cost of four-year education at a private college had exploded to $267,308—like buying a Lamborghini. The cost of a public university increased to $122,638. Duke University is more than $60,000 per year, and that's less than other schools.

While educational expense was rising, student competence for college success was declining. Millions of students have student loan debt without achieving a degree at all.

In no other nation but America do students have the opportunity that exists here—provided you perform. The ACT is a leading criterion for determining who wins the academic scholarships. One result of incompetence: billions of dollars of available scholarships go unclaimed each year, with many students unqualified or declining even the minimal effort to apply.

These students become easy prey. They receive student loans for a college education beyond their competence. They may finish but without a STEM major, their work doesn't pay enough to pay the loan payments.

As a result, student debt has grown 511 percent since 1999. This problem will haunt the economy for decades to come. Most of this was paid with student loans. Student loan debt now exceeds the nation's total auto and credit card debt. This is another cost of incompetence.

While student debt increased 24 percent, a degree could be acquired with minimal effort or stress. As long as it got them into good paying jobs they were willing to pay the increased cost. It conferred legitimacy and prestige. It was accepted by employers and society as an accomplishment; its absence still carried a stigma and considerable economic penalty.

While average student debt load increased 24 percent in the last decade, average wages for graduates ages 25 to 34 decreased 15 percent. In 2011, 53 percent of graduates under 25 were unemployed or underemployed.

ON CHOOSING A COLLEGE

Hear this: college is an investment of time and money from which a student should expect intellectual and economic gain. The reality is, however, right now most often parents allow their child to choose the college they will attend without guiding the child. t.Lab informs parents on choosing the right college with our own interactive tool for our students which uses nine evaluation criteria.

A new perspective about college selection must occur which enables students to choose wisely and avoid the pitfalls made in recent years. t.Lab developed the top nine criteria for choosing a college to help parents and students make their evaluations; the criteria are in order of importance.

These criteria enable the family to choose wisely. Rather than hoping for admission to any college, the student equipped for the choice can find the right fit for them. "How do I find the answers to these questions?" parents and students often ask. The answer is simple really: ask.

Each of the criterion below has a question you can ask, and a place you can get the answer from someone at the university. You can inquire of the teachers and students currently at the school. Ask the teachers about competition in classrooms and ask current students if the faculty loves teaching. Ask admissions about the scholarships available; ask the placement office who recruits at the school.

The number one factor when selecting a college must be the college's academic competition among the students. When students compete academically, students learn. So bar none, that's the number one factor.

The second factor is the love the college faculty has for teaching. Obviously, students want to learn from faculty who love teaching. The faculty exhibit their love for teaching students in two ways. The tenured faculty are teaching more than researching, and they have meaningful office hours when students can visit with them.

Our third factor reflects my previous statements about the differentiation of learning objectives from performance objectives. Performance in application enhances learning and its retention. The third criterion for a college is its availability of cooperative learning and internships. The former should be weighted more heavily because it gives a head start on the student's career, with relationship connections and additional resumé enhancement.

The fourth factor in importance for college selection is how much money the institution receives for research and development. Funding for research and development is important because it tells you if the school will be able to invest in future technologies.

A healthy expenditure in this area means your student will be exposed to new technology.

Number five: who recruits at the school? That tells you you're in the right place.

Criterion number six tells you if there are dollars for scholarships. However, this is not equivalent in importance to the factors above.

Number seven is the opportunity to become a leader on the campus. Can the potential student envision themselves as a leader on campus? It is crucial for a student to be able to envision himself or herself as a leader. Will they be comfortable enough to grow and exhibit leadership on campus?

The eighth factor is the college's leadership in the student's field of interest. Does the school or its faculty publish in the student's major area? Ask whether the school is currently doing research in the student's major, and whether they are known for research in this area. A signal of this is the starting pay of its graduates in that field, relative to the graduates of other colleges in the same field.

Lastly, the security on campus is an important consideration. Learning and the focus required can be impaired if a student doesn't feel safe.

Overall, these are the important factors to consider when selecting a college. But we are not reared to select colleges based on these factors. In our society, selection is determined by the student's feelings and emotions ("I want to go to a college that I like," and so forth). In reality, these emotion-based decisions should have nothing to do with college selection. Academic competition is cardinal. You could have the lousiest teachers in the world, but when students compete academically, learning and progress is going to happen.

What does student competition look like? Well, students who compete are vocal in discussing subjects and topics including issues surrounding leadership. They don't hide their voice; they are vocal. Competitive students are creative and have discussions in the classroom. And as they speak, the knowledge becomes reality in the mind.

Student competition then becomes a model for how the classroom should be. So in these particular cases, students come to class prepared. These students have study plans. This is a model for what has to happen.

Whether or not a student's friends will attend should not the be a determining factor when selecting a college. Once in college students develop new relationships, and choices matter greatly.

CHOICES IN COLLEGE: FROM 4.0 TO 3.4

One exemplary student's journey into college illustrated the power of focus and discipline in achieving academic success. The excellence continued for his first two years. During the freshman and sophomore years at his Tier 1 college, he maintained a perfect 4.0 GPA even with a rigorous course load, and permitted himself few outside distractions.

However, upon becoming a junior, the student began to cultivate new relationships, such as pledging a fraternity and beginning a romantic relationship. With the addition of these distractions, the student's GPA fell to 3.4 by the end of the year.

This is a stark contrast from the 4.0 of his previous semesters, and evidences the importance of focus and discipline for academic success. For students to excel in the classroom, it is essential that they remain focused and disciplined in their studies, no matter what else may be calling for their attention. Investing the time and energy into setting priorities can pay off tremendously, as this college student's story has shown us.

His example shows how quickly academic results can change if focus is lost. A 3.4 GPA is still impressive, but to lower from his previous 4.0 to a 3.4 involved mediocre performances and grades. Had he maintained the same level of focus and discipline, his perfect 4.0 could have carried through his college years. Therefore, for students hoping to reach their maximum academic potential, it is important to remain disciplined and focused on their studies in order to realize the best results.

Institutions of higher learning are often seen as a place to make friends, join clubs, start relationships, etc., but these outside activities should still be balanced with a commitment to one's education. Achieving high grades is a difficult task requiring dedication, focus, and discipline. As this college student's story shows, distractions have real consequences on academic performance.

If students don't understand and dedicate themselves to their studies, our country will not have the young people who can reverse the current trends. The needed levels of academic success will elude those who exhibit such distractions as this student. Commitment to one's studies can be difficult, especially with the many other activities that college has to offer. However, by remaining focused and disciplined in the pursuit of one's academic goals, great results can be achieved.

Ultimately, it is up to the individual student to find their own balance between focusing on their studies and engaging in outside activities. With the right amount of dedication and focus, a college student can achieve impressive results in their academic career—just like this college student did!

CHOICES IN COLLEGE: MENTORS

The most fruitful productive relationships are based on academics, which often will last forever. I remember somebody who was much better than I was and helped me through this process. I believe all students should have an adult, a parent or mentor help them choose the right college.

But we don't teach our young people based on our experiences. They aren't taught to value and leverage the experiences of their adult mentors. Although older, wiser voices can help them make better choices, our culture now says and believes young people should only listen to young people.

This is a mistake. Why not rely on the advice of someone who's been in the market, someone who's experienced the workforce in their major? Such people who are now mature understand the nuances of the field and the market. These older, experienced folks cannot be sold a bunch of baloney. You have to get them to work really hard to get them to spend their money.

Markets do not like experience; markets want easy marks. They want people they can lead easily. Markets say, "Hey, if you smoke this cigarette, you're going to be a famous celebrity," and everybody knows it's not true. Right? So what happens when the young and immature lead themselves? The sad reality is that our lack of wisdom is facilitating a dumb culture. And as Thomas Jefferson recognized, democracy's survival requires an educated public.

CHAPTER 12

CONCLUSION

We have a crisis: the students produced by the Mountain of Education are losing competence annually.

This presents our opportunity, and our accountability. With a receptivity to innovative educational technology, we can transform our educational output and reverse the decline of competency. Equity and inclusion can thrive when competence is the foundation. With our best team on the field, our students can learn more and manifest the achievements commensurate with diligence, character, and community. The dreams of Dr. Martin Luther King Jr. can be realized for our society.

The opportunity is in fact our accountability. Will we insist rigidly on perpetuating the old paradigms? If so, the gulf between student potential and student achievement will only widen. The present superior influence from arts and entertainment will amplify and accelerate. The Mountain of Business will leave our youth behind and recruit the qualified students produced by competing nations. And the security of our nation will continue to suffer.

Americans put men on the moon. African Americans transformed our society. A society of increasing literacy, character, and competence developed the freest nation of history. Our generations have repeatedly brought peace and transformed theaters of war into opportunities across the whole world. Educators sacrificed to produce the most advanced nation in history—so far. The achievements of our forebears ripple today throughout our daily lives.

But we can be freer. Fairness and justice can be broader. Innovative solutions for modern challenges can multiply more rapidly than ever with digital competencies.

All these are latent within our students. We can and must reverse our crisis of competence into an explosion of our students' potential.

We have come to see that the root cause of problems affecting urban cities and their education systems are systemic. While there is no one-size-fits-all solution, t.Lab has demonstrated that with rigorous academic standards and a focus on academic excellence, students in these areas can become extremely competitive and perform within the top 1% of all students in the US. This achievement is notable, especially considering that African American students are typically underrepresented in academic excellence.

We now know that with a focused effort on improving education systems, urban cities can make progress towards becoming more competitive and allowing their students to reach success and excel academically. We have seen that t.Lab's strategies are highly effective in helping students reach top performance levels. With ongoing support from both schools and communities, we can create brighter futures for students everywhere.

The work of t.Lab has proven that excellence is achievable no matter where you come from or what challenges you face. By setting a higher standard for academic excellence, we can pave the way for students of all backgrounds to reach their full potential. As A Crisis of Competence so clearly shows, with hard work and dedication, our education system can create the leaders of tomorrow.

As for the African American community, it is clear that there is still much work to be done to bring academic excellence and competitiveness. We must strive for our children to perform at the top 1% level within their respective cities and states. This can only be accomplished by implementing programs that offer the necessary support and resources to ensure excellence in education.

The Drive to 25 initiative is one such program that seeks to improve median ACT scores among African Americans through systems that integrate character, academic rigor, timely metrics, technology, and anointed teaching. This project will undoubtedly have profound implications for not just the African American community but all people who lack the insights to excel in education.

The need for greater access to quality education is an urgent one, and it is only through collective efforts that we will be able to make progress. We must work together towards a brighter future where all students are given equal opportunity regardless of race and socio-economic status. We may not be able to solve this issue overnight, but with dedication and perseverance, we can reach a point where academic excellence for all is within our grasp.

Let us never forget that the future of our nation depends on the success of its youth. Dr. Thomas Sowell has said, "You cannot measure opportunity by outcomes."* Our nation provides the most educational opportunity of any nation. The challenge is not lack of opportunity, but rather, enabling all students to maximize the opportunities that they have.

It is through education that we will be able to make lasting change and create an equitable society in which everyone has the opportunity to reach their potential. In this spirit, let us strive together toward a future of academic excellence and competitiveness for all members of our society.

Thank you for reading *A Crisis of Competence*! I hope that this book has served as a valuable resource in understanding the root-cause problems within the American education system supporting urban cities. Together, we can continue to drive the necessary change to bring about a brighter future for all.

Sincerely,

Your Friend and Guide.

Dr. Clarence Nixon Jr., Author

*Dr. Thomas Sowell, Wealth, Poverty, and Outcomes.

APPENDIX ONE

Performance in Secondary and Post-Secondary Standardized Tests by Race/Ethnicity

TEST / EXAM	AFRICAN AMERICAN	AMERICAN INDIAN / ALASKA NATIVE	WHITE	HISPANIC / LATINO	ASIAN	NATIVE HAWAIIAN / OTHER PACIFIC ISLANDER	TWO OR MORE RACES	NO RESPONSE / UNKNOWN
ACT – 2022								
Composite Score (max: 36)	16.1	16.4	21.3	17.7	24.7	17.1	20.1	17.6
Met All Benchmarks	5%	6%	29%	11%	51%	10%	12%	14%
	7,679	644	205,596	23,123	27,777	298	7,720	20,219
No. of Test Takers	153,579	10,728	708,952	210,205	54,464	2,961	64,390	144,425
SAT – 2022								
Mean Score (max 1600)	926	936	1,098	964	1,229	945	1,102	983
% Met All Benchmarks	19%	22%	53%	26%	75%	24%	52%	31%
No. of Test Takers	201,645	14,800	732,946	396,422	178,468	3,376	68,702	146,319
MCAT – 2022								
Mean Score (max 528)	497.4	498.7	507.9	500.1	509.2	502	505.4	508.5
No. of Test Takers	4,924	94	22,917	3,257	12,736	62	6,086	1,777
LSAT – 2017-2018								
Mean Score (max 180)	141.70	145.17	153.18	145.84	152.85	144.54	149.84	154.43
No. of Test Takers	10,997	363	48,608	8,096	7,043	106	8,251	1,990
DAT – 2021								
Academic Average (max: 30)	18.64	18.26	18.84	NO DATA	19.56	18.39	17.73	NO DATA
No. of Test Takers	1,161	46	6,236	NO DATA	3,452	41	1,701	NO DATA
GMAT – 2022								
Mean Score (max: 800)	479	524	585	522	618	514	592	611
No. of Test Takers	1,919	209	14,138	2,225	4,850	126	458	148
GRE – 2022								
Verbal Reasoning (max: 170)	147.0	149.9	152.6	148.9	152.9	149.3	152.5	152.7
Quantitative Reasoning (max: 170)	144.2	147.8	150.5	146.6	154.2	148.3	150.1	151.6
Analytical Writing (max: 6)	3.4	3.6	4.0	3.6	4.1	3.8	3.9	3.9
No. of Test Takers	9,237	705	66,878	12,674	10,935	313	3,883	20,526

APPENDIX ONE

APPENDIX TWO

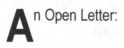

A n Open Letter:

FOUR QUESTIONS EVERY CORPORATION NEEDS TO ASK ABOUT THEIR CHARITABLE GIVING

We are at a major inflection point for societal transformation. As three African American males (including a former Police Chief and Deputy Mayor of a major city, a Chief Executive Officer, and a Senior Director with a total of five advanced college degrees), we see opportunity.

There is an opportunity today for making real the dreams of American freedom for everyone, especially African Americans. We acknowledge, and are inspired by, corporate America's recent commitments to diversity and inclusion. We also believe corporations can be catalysts for racial justice by engaging more intentionally in education-related charitable organizations and community groups.

But companies need first to stimulate change from the traditional metrics for assessing academic success. Second, they must invest in organizations that have a demonstrated record of success in the community. Third, corporations can demand measurable accountability from charitable organizations. The impact of money donated to charities should be measured. Fourth, corporate giving can encourage collaboration and shared goals among community-based organizations dedicated to educating students of color.

Last year, Americans gave more than $470 billion to charity. Fifteen percent of that, or about $71 billion, went toward education-related institutions and charities. Although monetary support for causes is praiseworthy, it does not ensure success. Some charities receive donations with little accountability or results, yet they garner most financial support targeted at minority communities, especially the African American community. On the other hand, there are a few organizations with high success rates, but they are too often underfunded.

https://givingusa.org/wp-content/uploads/2021/06/GUSA2021_Infographic_Digital.pdf

Despite the influx of money into education—both through charitable giving and government funding—academic performance among all students, especially African Americans, continues to drop.

Nationally, standardized test scores are falling; and African Americans are performing the lowest at the secondary level and beyond (e.g., the ACT, SAT, LSAT, DAT, MCAT, GMAT, and GRE). Students are woefully unprepared to take on higher education or tech-based jobs. As a result of these challenges, students, especially students of color, are being left behind in the fields of STEM (science, technology, engineering, and math) that are necessary for economic growth and maintaining competitiveness in today's modern world.

Figure 1: ACT Performance by Race/Ethnicity, Percent of Students that Met All Benchmarks

Student Group	Race/Ethnicity	N	English %	Mathematics %	Reading %	Science %	All Four %	STEM %
	All Students	1,295,349	56	36	44	35	26	19
National	Black/African American	153,641	28	10	18	11	6	3
	American Indian/Alaska Native	10,094	30	13	22	14	7	5
	White	698,565	67	44	53	44	31	24
	Hispanic/Latino	181,968	41	22	31	22	14	10
	Asian	54,272	76	67	64	61	52	44
	Native Hawaiian/Other Pacific Islander	3,450	33	16	23	16	11	8
	Two or More Races	58,538	58	35	45	36	25	18
	Prefer Not to Respond	134,641	46	20	36	29	20	16

As a recent article in Quillette described, the United States is losing ground competitively to nations like China. We already rely on a continual inflow of foreign talent, particularly from mainland China, Taiwan, South Korea, and India. As evidence, the National Foundation for American Policy estimated that international students accounted for 88 percent of full-time graduate students in electrical engineering at US universities; and 78 percent of full-time graduate students in computer and information sciences. As well, according to the National Science Foundation, between 2001 and 2016, the proportion of bachelor's degrees awarded to African Americans declined from 5 to 4 percent in engineering and from 7 to 4 percent in math—despite labor demand growth in STEM fields. [https://quillette.com/2021/08/19/as-us-schools-prioritize-diversity-over-merit-china-is-becoming-the-worlds-stem-leader/]

[https://nfap.com/wp-content/uploads/2021/08/International-Students-in-Science-and-Engineering.NFAP-Policy-Brief.August-2021.pdf]

[https://ncses.nsf.gov/pubs/nsf19304/digest/field-of-degree-minorities]

While corporations and educational institutions have responded to the need for diversity and inclusion by establishing new infrastructure, it is time to invest in programs that develop STEM skills among students, especially African Americans. We believe corporate America can provide leadership for change in education through targeted charitable giving that prioritizes competence and success.

Demand for "return on investment" or results from charitable organizations is typically low or non-existent, which directly affects the sense of urgency in tackling the real issues in education—skill levels, character, and innovation. These three aspects are the foundation of success and advancement for all, especially minorities and African Americans.

The focus of many minority community organizations continues to be narrow in scope, such as only focusing on the issue of high school graduation, entry into college, and college debt. These measurements fail to address the root cause for the lack of academic success. It is not clear why such a narrow scope persists despite the evidence of fruitlessness. Clearly, more of the same is not yielding measurable results that count.

Corporate America is missing an opportunity to transform the nation (and ultimately the world) by not investing in programs and organizations with demonstrated success in preparing African Americans. A few examples are Sage Group America in Bastrop, Louisiana (college preparation); MKE Fellows in Milwaukee, Wisconsin (character and leadership development); and ITSMF (Information Technology Senior Management Forum, focused on professional development in the workplace).

Not to mention my own t.Lab, which has a lengthy track record of increasing the competence of all students, including African American ones.

By not adopting meaningful metrics for measuring outcomes that are consistent for all, corporate America is abdicating its fiduciary responsibility to its shareholders and stakeholders.

Corporate giving that disdains those organizations proven to produce competence and human capital only sustains the status quo, which no one desires. The lip service given to diversity and inclusion by such corporate giving will remain a mirage.

In closing, these are the questions corporations should ask themselves:

1. Are we committed to changing academic success for African Americans?

2. Do we invest in successful community organizations with demonstrated success in the community?
3. Do we expect quantified results from organizations we contribute to?
4. Do we encourage collaboration and common goals among community-based organizations that educate students of color?

We are encouraged by the corporate efforts to bring about a diverse and inclusive society. However, these efforts will fall short of their intended goals, without integrating high academic performance standards and competency. This can be measured for all; it is especially critical for African American students and those serving them. We are certain that America will grow and increase its competitiveness and its impact on the world.

---Dr. Clarence Nixon Jr.

– Founder and CEO, Technology Laboratory and Professional Development Center (t.Lab)

APPENDIX THREE

THE PENALTY OF LEADERSHIP*
By Theodore MacManus

*This text appeared as an advertisement in The Saturday Evening Post, January 2nd, in the year 1915. Copyright, Cadillac Motor Car Company.

In every field of human endeavor, he that is first must perpetually live in the white light of publicity. Whether the leadership be vested in a man or in a manufactured product, emulation and envy are ever at work. In art, in literature, in music, in industry, the reward and the punishment are always the same. The reward is widespread recognition; the punishment, fierce denial and detraction.

When a man's work becomes a standard for the whole world, it also becomes a target for the shafts of the envious few. If his work be merely mediocre, he will be left severely alone—if he achieves a masterpiece, it will set a million tongues a-wagging. Jealousy does not protrude its forked tongue at the artist who produces a commonplace painting. Whatsoever you write, or paint, or play, or sing, or build, no one will strive to surpass or to slander you, unless your work be stamped with the seal of genius.

Long, long after a great work or a good work has been done, those who are disappointed or envious continue to cry out that it cannot be done. Spiteful little voices in the domain of art were raised against our own Whistler as a mountebank, long after the big world had acclaimed him its greatest artistic genius. Multitudes flocked to Bayreuth to worship at the musical shrine of Wagner, while the little group of those whom he had dethroned and displaced argued angrily that he was no musician at all. The little world continued to protest that Fulton could never build a steamboat, while the big world flocked to the riverbanks to see his boat steam by.

The leader is assailed because he is a leader, and the effort to equal him is merely added proof of that leadership. Failing to equal or to excel, the follower seeks to depreciate and to destroy—but only confirms once more the superiority of that which he strives to supplant.

There is nothing new in this. It is as old as the world and as old as the human passions—envy, fear, greed, ambition, and the desire to surpass. And it all avails nothing. If the leader truly leads, he re-mains—the leader. Master-poet, master-painter, master-workman, each in his turn is assailed, and each holds his laurels through the ages. That which is good or great makes itself known, no matter how loud the clamor of denial. That which deserves to live—lives.

(From *Sunrise Magazine*, January 1952; copyright © 1952 Theosophical University Press)